Musical Violence

Gangsta Rap and Politics in Sierra Leone

Boima Tucker

NORDISKA AFRIKAINSTITUTET, UPPSALA 2013

INDEXING TERMS:
Sierra Leone
Youth
Popular music
Politics
Social change
Cultural identity

Language editing: Peter Colenbrander
ISSN 0280-2171
ISBN 978-91-7106-734-0
© The author and Nordiska Afrikainstitutet 2013
Production: Byrå4
Print on demand, Lightning Source UK Ltd.

Contents

New digital technology has made music production simpler and cheaper. This has meant radical changes across the world, since anyone with a computer, a few programs (frequently pirated) and without even knowing how to play an instrument can produce music. These changes formed the basis for a Sierra Leonean music revolution that took off after the end of the country's civil war (1991-2002). In the aftermath of the war, Sierra Leonean music flooded the capital Freetown and the entire country and also made serious inroads in neighbouring Liberia. At the height of their popularity (2005-07), Sierra Leonean musicians completely dominated the airwaves. The music drew inspiration from pop in the global North and the Caribbean but typically blended in local and sub-regional influences. Young and old danced to the music, listened and commented on the lyrics. Quite often, new slang on the streets of Freetown drew on popular lyrics. For a time, everybody took an interest, filling the national stadium and turning young Sierra Leonean female and male artists into superstars. The lyrics dealt with love and the other things most music is about, but there was a special genre that people at the time took especially seriously, called by some conscious music and by others revolutionary music. Artists sang about the hardships of everyday life, about corrupt politicians and the way things ought to work. To many, these songs were more objective than news media. Then musicians started to be coopted by politicians, CD piracy destroyed the profitability of the business and some of the best-known musicians moved to greener pastures in the global North. This doesn't mean Sierra Leonean music is dead. There is still a lot of interesting music, music that at times still manages to unsettle politics and, more tragically, local order, as was proved in April 2013 in the riots that followed the banning of a concert by Sierra Leone hip-hop icon Kao Denero.

Boima Tucker is himself a musician, a writer and an academic. The son of Sierra Leonean parents, he grew up in the US. In this study, he sets out to understand the wider politics of music and music-making in Sierra Leone. Few are better placed to do so or as knowledgeable about the field.

Uppsala 15 April 2013

Mats Utas
Head of the cluster on Conflict, security and democratic transformation at NAI, long-term researcher in Sierra Leone and former music producer in that country.

Mi Yone Music

I grew up the son of a Sierra Leonean immigrant in the United States, and as with many children of a diaspora, music played a central role in the celebration of my own cultural identity. I absorbed Sierra Leonean culture while outside the country through family and community gatherings. Whenever we would gather for any kind of event, food, music and fashion were always central to the occasion, and these elements came to form the basis of my connection to my father's homeland. My experience of cultural immersion only intensified after relatives fleeing the civil conflict in Sierra Leone arrived in the United States. In my teenage years, I lost touch with this culture as I explored American subcultures and formed an identity based on Hip Hop, Reggae and Electronic Dance Music. What I was not aware of at the time was that my age-mates in Sierra Leone were absorbing many of the same influences, blurring the distinctions flowing from conflict and physical distance. In 2006, when I finally was able to visit West Africa, I jumped at the opportunity to spend a few days with family in Freetown. By this point, music had become a career interest of mine and remained at the centre of my life. So, upon arrival, and quickly realising the central role music played in people's everyday lives, I felt a warm sense of belonging in a *new* place I had always thought of as *home*.

On the streets of Freetown, I was astonished to find live music woven into the daily life of the city, as brass marching bands blocked traffic and traditional drums celebrated life's milestones, such as births or weddings, in a very public way, rather than in the closed manner I had experienced in the diaspora. At the same time, I noticed a very vibrant global urban youth culture that reminded me of cities I had visited around the world, such as Kingston, New York or London. Blaring out of cars and around the streets at music sellers' stands, local variations of Dancehall, contemporary Highlife, R&B, Zouk and Hip Hop were all the rage. In a local club, I was amazed to come across a diverse selection of musical styles ranging from places as far removed as Senegal, Puerto Rico, England and Jamaica. Exposure to all this music in a place I had assumed was, due to war, disconnected from global pop cultural conversations was exciting, but I had yet to understand the meaning of what was really happening around me.

It was my uncle, who at the time was working as a government minister, who inadvertently gave me some insight into the dynamics at play on the streets of Freetown. While driving (or rather sitting in traffic) on Kissi Road in Freetown's East End, we passed stand after stand blaring music, with young people watching over stacks of tapes and CDs. My uncle just shook his head and said there was too much noise on the streets. He dismissed the young people with an attitude that suggested they were out of control. The familiarity of his reaction surprised me, as it echoed my father's reaction to my own music in the US. I protested: "But this is my music too!" He shrugged. I had always associated the difference in taste between my father and me to a generational gap and the cultural differences that inevitably emerge between an immigrant and his children. Here, the same dynamic was being played out on the streets between people of and from the same place.

On my return to the US equipped with a few CDs, I started to engage with the locally produced music further. After analysing some of the lyrics, I noticed a keen sense of global connectivity. The introduction to the Baw Waw Society's 2005 album *Fertilizer* exemplifies this by exclaiming "this goes out to all Sierra Leoneans at home and abroad!" Difficult to miss alongside this global orientation was a hyper-awareness among some artists of the many social ills that existed in Sierra Leone. In the biggest hit songs of the time, popular artists sang against government corruption, greed and wealth disparities. The popularity of these songs came to mark local audiences as particularly politically engaged. Western news agencies such as the BBC picked up on this and speculated that the local music scene would play an integral role in deciding the outcome of elections (Panton 2006). I started to become aware that around the globe Sierra Leonean music was becoming synonymous with youth political participation.

In the following years, my engagement with the music and desire to learn as much as I could about the scene led me to meet, befriend and even collaborate with several of the industry's prominent artists, including Khady Black, Black Nature, Bajah and the Dry Yai Crew, and Ahmed Janka Nabay. My world travels allowed me to meet Sierra Leoneans living all over the US, London, the rest of West Africa and even as far away as Australia. My comprehension of Krio, the local *lingua franca* had improved, as well as my knowledge of local politics. Food and music were no longer the sole definition of my Sierra Leonean identity. I was now fully engaged with, and part of, a community called the Sierra Leone diaspora, and I was excited by the notion that Sierra Leoneans had such a diverse global identity.

My second trip to Sierra Leone occurred in the summer of 2011. On this trip, my own lens on the country and the society changed considerably. Either because of my own changed perspective on the country or an actual change in society, I noticed a significant difference in the musical environment during this second visit. While the live music around cultural events, and a global mix of pop sounds remained, noticeably less prevalent were the local digital dance sounds thumping on every corner. While a few big Sierra Leonean artists' songs got played on the streets and in public transport, most of the songs were by people living abroad in England or the US, and the songs were primarily about love and material wealth. I got a sense that the previously vibrant, politically engaged local music had somehow died.

In asking people around town for their thoughts on why the musical environment had changed so much, the responses varied according to whether they were consumers or fans of the music, or producers or musical artists. A common explanation by consumers I met, especially a group of journalists, was that the political music of the past was no longer relevant because all the artists had been co-opted by politicians. Even Emmerson, the one artist said to have retained some integrity by continuing to make protest songs, had been neutralised by the party propaganda machine as the result of an intricate game of ethnic partisanship being played out among the public. Consumers also criticised the quality of local music, saying that it wasn't as good as the Afro-pop sounds coming out of mainly Nigeria, or globally oriented sounds coming out of the US, United Kingdom and Jamaica.

On the other hand, for artists bootlegging was a major concern, and in their minds was a central reason for the downturn in local production. In the summer of 2011, cultural producers from all types of media seemed to place the overwhelm blame for problems in local media industries on piracy (Hansen 2012). In previous years, many cassette sellers had been attacked by artists for selling bootleg copies of their music, and because of this intimidation opted not to sell local music. Beyond preferring a better production aesthetic, Sierra Leonean consumers also had better access to foreign music, which could be freely pirated and distributed without immediate backlash from the artists. While I was in Freetown, the government happened to pass Sierra Leone's first anti-piracy law, to the delight of many media creators in the country. Several months after the passage of the law, my nephew reported to me that music vendors were just continuing to not sell locally produced music.

All this focus on piracy by artists seemed a bit misdirected to me. As Michael Stasik argues, piracy may have contributed to the boom in local music due to its increased availability through digital copying (2011: 66–7). Additionally, copyright law theorist Larisa Mann argues that copyright opens the door to a dubious world of intellectual property regulation that could pave over local ideas of cultural exchange (2011). The question of piracy and intellectual property, increasingly relevant across the globe, inevitably comes down to the question of who is making money, and whether it's fairly distributed. So I wondered whether there were other dynamics at play that weren't as evident on the surface.

A conversation I had with popular rapper YOK 7 gives a little insight into why money is such an important determinant of the health of the local industry, beyond the material resources needed for production. He said that when an artist has a popular hit and his music is played everywhere, his friends and family assume that he is profiting from it in some way. In Freetown society, where there is scarcely any formal social safety net, one gets by on reciprocity within families and networks of friends. One day you buy lunch for a friend, the next he or she will buy dinner for you. In an environment where money is easy come, easy go, these social networks are a means of survival. When one's social circle is connected by a web of interdependence, and the others in that circle think the artist has money, they expect that person to provide for them. If that person doesn't have money and is in need, the others in the social circle will refuse to provide the help they may previously have given. Commercial success without financial reward leaves artists marginalised within their network of social support. This prevents even those who might make music for other reasons, such as for fun or to make a political statement, from doing so. Intrigued by the cultural explanations I was coming across during that visit, I decided to dig deeper in my research when I got back to the US.

Further Investigations

Contemporary Sierra Leone has an outward-looking music culture increasingly integrated into a global market of pop consumption and fuelled by mobile phones, digital media and the Internet. For good or bad, advances in digital technology have caused a multitude of changes in local culture in a short period. With the arrival of broadband in 2012, the coming years will only see an acceleration in these changes. To survive, local artists will have to continue to adapt. For years, Sierra Leone has had a rich, vibrant and globally informed youth culture. It was this cultural milieu that facilitated a boom in the local music industry between the end of the civil war in 2002 and the national elections in 2007. Yet global market and cultural pressures, compounded by digital communication, have forced popular Sierra Leonean music artists and media creators to leave the country to seek their fortunes abroad. Places like Nigeria, Ghana, the US or the UK have long symbolised (yet have not always delivered) a better future and more access to resources for Sierra Leoneans of all backgrounds. Locally, with increased access to information for even the most marginalised street youth, the allure of these places has only intensified. It is in this context that we can locate a new youth cultural aesthetic emerging in the country.

In the wake of the increased political importance of youth music during the elections of 2007, the post-election period has been marked by a decline in explicitly political musical content. Particularly notable is the rise of a scene influenced by American Gangsta Rap. Its accompanying aesthetics have become a preferred mode of self-expression and the basis for the formation of group identities among many young people in Sierra Leone. From the outside it seems that the oppositional youth identity, once so excited about holding politicians accountable to the masses, is now too consumed with materialism, sex, love, partying and so called intergroup "beef." Seemingly, instead of cultivating a local identity, Sierra Leonean artists are concentrating on creating audio and visual content that assimilates them into the global pop cultural complex.

Yet these approximations to global pop and the appropriation of Gangsta Rap should not simply be interpreted as a form of cultural imperialism, or a global flattening of culture. Such cultural manifestations have a lot to tell us about local socio-cultural forces as well. Stretching back to the 1990s in the middle of the civil war, the Gangsta Rap aesthetic served as a convenient channel through which Sierra Leonean youth could express their views on their place in society (Prestholdt 2009). Today, popular Sierra Leonean artists, whether based at home or abroad, become nodes for participants to gather around in this globally informed youth lifestyle. It is when these artists appear in public that Sierra Leone's marginalised youth are especially able to assert their belonging in an increasingly global society.

What I will attempt throughout this paper is to flesh out the political meaning contained within contemporary youth culture in Sierra Leone, and the adaptation of gangster aesthetics in a post-conflict society. I argue that this music and violence are forms of political dissent that address two contexts, a global one in which a dichotomy between the West and Africa is played out, and a local one informed by a desire for social mobility and the right to be recognised as political speakers. In local media reports on the appearance of violence in the public sphere, journalists often speculate about who is responsible – wayward youth, the musicians they follow or self-serving politicians? In contrast, I argue that violence and a disruption of the social order in Sierra Leone is a form of political speech for marginalised youth, and arises regardless of the intentions of the figures in whose name it is carried out. My thesis is that in Sierra Leone politics happens in the space between the state's attempt to enact an internationally prescribed social order and its failure to address the demands of a subaltern identity called youth. Throughout Sierra Leonean history, this space has been occupied by an alternation between cultural production and violence, and sometimes by a merging of the two.

My paper will focus on youth music and politics in Sierra Leone after the election of 2007. This period marks a distinct shift in the political landscape of the country for a couple of reasons. First, it was the end of the term limits for the incumbent president, Ahmad Tejan Kabbah, and the peaceful transfer of power through the ballot box would be a first for the country. Second, this being only the second election since the end of the civil war, it was held up as an important barometer of the health of Sierra Leone's democracy and the international community's liberal peace-building project. A reasonably peaceful transfer of power through elections would signal to the international community that Sierra Leone had successfully recovered and was on the track to development. This period also marked a distinct shift in the cultural landscape, for it was the point at which the booming local music industry seemingly fell apart. Soon after this downturn, the local industry saw the increasing shift in sites of production from local studios to various globally dispersed diaspora locations, as well as the shift in taste among music audiences and consumers from mostly local to global musical output. Finally, this period also saw the re-emergence of youth-perpetrated violence in the public sphere.

The literature I reviewed and the research I undertook for this paper comes from academic analysis, popular media and the personal opinions of people I interviewed or interacted with. These forms of information can give a well-rounded view of how people interpret different forms of speech and their political meaning. Generally, published academic scholarship is based in the West, so there is a need to gather information from popular sources on how average Sierra Leoneans view political meaning in various social realms. To get an idea of the current relationship between music and politics in Sierra Leone, I consulted popular media sources, such as local newspaper websites and Youtube videos. I then base my analysis on field observations and relate it back to the theoretical analyses of other scholars.

Sierra Leone in the Global Imagination

To orient the analysis of youth cultural production in Sierra Leone, we must begin by identifying the context in which contemporary global dialogues place the country. In the international media, Sierra Leone has often been a footnote in debates on African social issues. During the civil war, blood diamonds and child soldiering were popular topics that often fell under the spotlight in the international press. Attempts to make mainstream audiences more aware of the war and its issues, such as the Hollywood movie Blood Diamond and American recording artist Kanye West's song "Diamonds from Sierra Leone," came late and marginalised Sierra Leonean voices by placing Western protagonists at the centre of their narratives. Today, the narrative on Africa is changing from describing the continent as a place to send aid to one that sees it as a place for international investment. In this narrative, African cultural production, such as the film and music industries in Nigeria, are celebrated as signs of hope for the continent's development and integration into a global economic and political order. Yet Sierra Leone's inclusion in this wider narrative on Africa has been slow. International depictions of Sierra Leone continue to concentrate on social issues such as gender-based violence and maternal mortality rates. While Sierra Leone still has real social problems, the perpetuation of older narratives continues to deny Sierra Leonean agency in their solution. In a world of increasingly interconnected global communications, the circulation of media narratives that marginalise Sierra Leonean perspectives make their way back home, informing Sierra Leoneans' ideas of their place in global society.

Popular media hasn't been the only force shaping global perceptions of Sierra Leone. With the end of the Cold War, many people around the world celebrated the fading of the global ideological battle between the Soviet Union and the West. Conflicts that continued in the wake of the Cold War did so without clear ideological allegiances, and outside observers in places like Liberia and Sierra Leone struggled to find the political meaning behind them. A school of conservative Western academic thought saw the fall of the Communist bloc as proof of the supremacy of liberal democracy and free market capitalism. This school tried to locate the reasons for civil conflict in countries like Sierra Leone in their inability to install a proper system of liberal democratic governance and economic order. A theory advanced by Robert Kaplan was that in the post-Cold War period population explosions leading to stiff competition for resources, ecological degradation and renewal of deep-seated tribal animosities in countries on the margins of the global economy have naturally led to dissolution of the state and incomprehensible acts interpersonal violence (1994). Kaplan's thesis came to influence the post-Cold War foreign policies of many Western governments and to shape the international view of Sierra Leone as a backward, lawless country (Richards 1999).

Theorists such as Mary Moran, Stephen Ellis, Rosalind Shaw, Danny Hoffman, Mats Utas, Maya Christensen and Paul Richards worked to counter Kaplan's ideas. Richards, an anthropologist who undertook extensive investigations in Sierra Leone among rebel fighters during the war, dubbed Kaplan's thesis the theory of *New Barbarism* (1996). This name aimed to expose the logic behind Kaplan's theory as depending on notions of a non-civilised society or of the "cultural other" (Moran 2006: 23). These theorists went about investigating the meaning behind the violence to counter the idea that the root causes lay in a breakdown in Western prescribed ideas of social order. They suggested that violence resulted from everything from the spiritual organisation of the societies to an inherent relationship between violence and democracy in global politics. By doing this, they were able to restore the agency of Africans and their participation in the conflict, as well as provide alternative suggestions for addressing the crises. Yet, as Mary Moran suggests, even though disproving the three tenets Kaplan bases his theory on, they continue to leave their mark on international politics (2006: 15). Dismantling the logic of the cultural other behind New Barbarism, and the global media environment that propagates it, is especially relevant to our purposes, since this logic continues to inform the policy decisions that affect average Sierra Leoneans.

Owing to the central role of youth in the fighting in Liberia and Sierra Leone, an analysis of this role takes a prominent place in the New Barbarism discourse. Danny Hoffman uses Jaques Rancière's theory of dissensus to explain the political meaning of violence during the war (2006). The application of this theory to Sierra Leone is useful for understanding youth political participation in the society. Dissensus is a disruption of the normal orders of perception through which people or objects are distributed into their *proper* places. Rancière proposes this as a more representative form of democracy than consensus, the form of governance sponsored and enforced by the international peace-building regime in Sierra Leone after the civil war. Consensus functions in contemporary global society as a process of agreement among professional politicians. Through this process, some perspectives become automatically marginalised and remain excluded from the realm of the proper through various forms of *policing.* Dissensus is a form of democracy in which *new* subjects and heterogeneous objects are able to "stage the effects of equality," even outside official channels (Corcoran 2010: 7). Rancière says that these new ideas may become incorporated into the normal order of things, and that new subjectivities and heterogeneous objects may eventually arise. According to Hoffman, the use of unthinkably violent acts was a strategic political speech act that introduced new perceptions of *the possible* in Sierra Leonean society. Youth who participated in the fighting wanted to contest the order that determined their proper place in society and left them marginalised. Violent acts were forms of political speech through which youth were able to assert new notions of the distribution of power and social control in both a local and global context (Hoffman 2006). Today, young people across the world continue to be the most economically and politically marginalised in their societies. Increased access to information through digital communication has widened the gap between young people's expectations and their realities. This has led to an uprising of youth on every continent. In Sierra Leone, these gaps, and the lack of official channels to address them, continue to inform youth participation in the public sphere, whether through violence or other means.

Examining youth cultural production in Sierra Leone can give us further insight into how youths understood their place in society, and thus into participation in violent conflict. During the war, youth appropriation of an American Hip Hop aesthetic was documented in journalistic accounts of various battles. These depictions would continue to colour international representations of Sierra Leonean youth in the postwar years. A 2003 article published on the *Vice Magazine* website called "Gen. Butt Naked vs. The Tupac Army: West Africa Has Gone Mad and It Looks Fantastic!" sensationalised the appearance of American rap icons in the uniforms of child soldiers. In 2007, VH1 aired a documentary called *Bling! A Planet Rock* that tried to connect American rappers to conflict diamonds, Sierra Leone and local rappers, and involved bringing a group of popular American artists to postwar Sierra Leone. Mostly, these pieces provided a New Barbarism-informed account of ruthless teens running around committing atrocities, fuelled by drugs and Gangsta Rap. One popular book that did attempt to give a Sierra Leonean perspective on the war was Ishmael Beah's *A Long Way Gone* (2007), a memoir of his experience as a child soldier. Hip Hop plays a central role in his account as well. While Beah's account is insightful about his own perspective, it does not attempt to mine the meaning behind youth participation in the war, and thus fails to break the logic of an uncivilised other in the New Barbarism thesis.

While popular media continue to engage in New Barbarism-tinged representations of youth in these conflicts, academics have sought to find the local meanings behind young people's appropriation of American Rap aesthetics in Sierra Leone's civil war. Katrin Lock's essay "Who is Listening? Sierra Leone, Liberia, and Senegal," argued that child soldiers related to the representations of marginalised perspectives in the music, and thus appropriated it for their own purposes (2005). Jeremy Prestholdt went further by drawing specific connections between the appropriation of American Rapper Tupac Shakur by rebel armies and their understanding of their place in society. He shows how as a mythical figure, Tupac was able to effect the coalescence of a transnational identity that was easily tailored to various local contexts of violence and social marginalisation. Rebel soldiers wore Tupac T-shirts, painted murals of him, added his slogans to their vehicles and loudly played his music as they rolled into battle. Prestholdt argues that Tupac gave Sierra Leonean youth rebels a notion of international belonging, a means through which to express their marginal position in society and a vehicle through which they could justify their participation in violence (2009). These attempts to demonstrate the deeper meaning behind the appropriation of Hip Hop aesthetics were a start in the efforts to demystify the ideas perpetuated by popular media sources.

While it is important to look at what such appropriation symbolises in order to understand Sierra Leonean youth's perspectives, it is also necessary to acknowledge the ways in which the appropriation of Hip Hop aesthetics has become a form of social navigation and political contestation. Jörgel and Utas's analysis of the military strategies of the West Side Boys rebel group allows for examination of the appropriation of Gangster Rap as a form of social and military navigation. These theorists suggest the appropriation of these aesthetics was a form of strategic manoeuvring during the war. One tactic known as *fearful yourself*, the adoption of a fearful Gangster Rap look and aesthetic, was a mode of psychological warfare to reduce resistance when trying to take villages (Utas and Jörgel 2008). Instead of having to constantly use brute force, the rebels understood that to take a town, sometimes they just had to evoke the aura of fearfulness associated with Gangster Rap and other foreign aesthetics by the civilian population.

After the end of the war in 2002, there was a shift in the forms of youth political participation, as well as in modes of engagement by Sierra Leonean youth with Hip Hop. Susan Shepler analyses the elections of 2007, when local music production took centre stage in Sierra Leonean political life. During this time, the youth regularly expressed their grievances through music and were able to voice the desire for political change that was growing among the general population. Initially, mainstream politicians didn't really take youth music seriously, in keeping with their general attitude towards the youth population. However, the popularity of the music among a majority of the population made politicians pay attention to what the youth were saying. Thus, the political voice of youth was amplified through popular music audiences, and made both the international community and local politicians aware of the perspectives of a subaltern population. Shepler argues this awareness signalled a clear continuity between violent rebellion and cultural production in the strategy of youth to intervene in state politics and national discourse (2010).

While it was easy to identify the ways in which young people were actively engaged in national discourse before 2007, after the elections of that year the Sierra Leonean music industry saw a decline in the popularity of locally produced music. This made it more difficult to recognise any explicitly political project among Sierra Leonean youth. Borrowing from musicologist Christopher Small, Stasik argues that a shift from analysing the lyrics and content of the music to analysing the musicking practices among the Sierra Leonean public is necessary to get a sense of the social forces at work in the country. He suggests that a major reason for the decline in the industry is due to "politics fatigue" among the general public. This fatigue has caused music audiences to shift attention from the public realm and to engage with music that concerns the private realm. He identifies "love music" (a globally oriented music that is individualistic and aspirational) as the realm in which the hopes and desires of the young generation in Freetown are manifested today. This music allows them to temporarily imagine a pathway to social advancement and transgressing social barriers, yet the constraints arising from the organisation of Sierra Leonean society mean that many of these dreams cannot be fulfilled (2011: 152-5). While this analysis is good at identifying some of the social forces affecting the current state of music in Sierra Leone, it ignores the political project that does arise in Sierra Leonean youth musicking practices. As Rancière's logic shows, politics seeks to blur the lines between what belongs to the public realm and what belongs to the private sphere. By playing out their dreams *en masse* through their musical choices, Sierra Leonean youth are introducing into public discourse a new possibility for the country's future. Even though their concerns have turned inward, they remain firmly in the realm of a politics of dissensus.

Today, Sierra Leone is recognised by the international media and policymakers as at peace. In the wake of a massive international peace-building effort, the country is characterised as an emerging democracy with a relatively peaceful transition between rival parties in 2007. Yet, while the international community generally champions the successful installation of a liberal democratic governance model, a spectre of violence hangs over the society. This spectre leads many commentators to question whether the national peace in Sierra Leone is stable (Adolfo 2010). The consensus form of governance advocated by the international peace-building regime puts career politicians belonging to the major political parties at the centre of political discourse. At the same time, an informal system of political navigation based on social structures hardened throughout the colonial era persists under the cover of liberal democracy (Utas 2012). Inevitably, those voices marginalised from these mainstream systems of governance will find a way to be heard. Whether those voices make themselves heard through violence or not depends largely on the modes of policing employed by the authorities.

The various forms of political speech existing in Sierra Leone are shaped by the persistent denial of equal membership in both global and local society for a significant part of the population (Fanthorpe 2001). Expanding on analyses of Sierra Leonean politics and modes of social navigation during wartime, I attempt to identify the manifestations of political speech in the country during peacetime. By doing this, I challenge those observers who suggest that the forms of political speech that existed during and directly after the war have disappeared. I suggest that in the face of the continued marginalisation of Sierra Leonean voices from the international sphere, the forms of political speech that have arisen have been informed by a more globally oriented worldview. I will expand on Susan Shepler's suggestion that music was able to partly supplant violence as a form of youth political participation during the elections of 2007, and suggest there is a constant shifting between violence and music as forms of political speech, partly as a result of policing by the ruling regime. While manipulation by political parties has neutralised the oppositional potential of explicitly political music in Sierra Leone, the shifting of political speech between cultural production and violence creates a hybrid form of implicit political speech that merges the two. Today, this is most clearly manifested in the Gangsta Rap culture, a sort of musical-violence that has come to characterise the Sierra Leonean music industry and urban youth culture. I begin by looking at the origins of the formation of the Sierra Leone state and of the social structures that shape the forms of political speech. Then, starting in the prewar period, I look at the ways in which forms of political speech have shifted over time. Finally, I look at how the forms of political speech today are manifested through Gangsta Rap aesthetics.

In April of 2010, amid Sierra Leone's 49th independence anniversary celebrations, international pop singer Akon performed at the national stadium in Freetown. The son of a Senegalese musician, Akon emigrated to the US as a young boy. He has been able to manage an extremely successful career as an international music artist and label executive, and has since become an influential investor in several global industries, particularly in his home country of Senegal. Akon is arguably Africa's first international pop superstar, and has been immensely popular in Sierra Leone as far back as 2006. The star power of Akon in Freetown can be compared to The Beatles or Michael Jackson, and can be seen in the hysteria evident in a cellphone video shot by one of his entourage in which a frantic mob surrounds his car.[1] Importantly, this moment illustrates the extent to which music events can disrupt daily life in Freetown, and highlights the way in which youth gatherings can create the perception of chaos engulfing the city.

Akon's concert was significant for Sierra Leone in an international sense, because it recognised Freetown as an important node in the singer's mission to incorporate Africans into the global pop culture conversation. A series of videos shot during the concert and uploaded to Youtube by *We D Best Promo*, conveys the excitement of the crowd and the high energy surrounding the show. The first video begins by showing Akon's performance in the national stadium, and an enthusiastic crowd singing along with every word. The crowd's energy remains high in spite of the constant failures of the sound system.[2] At the end of his performance, Akon invites two of the most popular Sierra Leonean rappers on to the stage to perform their local hit songs. Part three of the series[3] starts out with a Sierra Leonean "beef" song taunting an unknown opponent not to mess with the rapper, who calls himself a "five star general," thus reflecting a self-naming practice common during the civil war. The video's producers are purposely setting us up for what is to follow. The action continues with Sierra Leonean rapper LAJ excitedly dancing on stage next to Akon. Both of them are holding microphones and LAJ is rapping his song "Money Nar Bank" while Akon plays hype-man. A red title at the bottom signals LAJ's crew "R-F-M" for the Red Flag Movement. The crowd's excited reaction clearly displays the pride in having a local star on stage with Akon. After a short clip of LAJ performing, the video cuts to another Sierra Leonean rapper, Kao Denero, who now holds the microphone with LAJ by his side. It's not clear how LAJ lost the microphone, but his song is still playing and he's visibly agitated.

The next part of the action is manipulated for the viewer by the video's pro-

1.   http://www.twitvid.com/KCN2M

2.   http://youtu.be/C3m9KPX3bbA

3.   http://youtu.be/1sMO1j15JU4

ducers to emphasise its importance. First, LAJ tries to grab the microphone away from Kao Denero, but Kao doesn't let him. Then the introductory "beef" music returns as a non-diegetic soundtrack played over the action of LAJ trying to grab the microphone. This action is repeated several times. The attempt by the video editor to draw the incident out and perhaps make it seem bigger than it really was highlights the importance Sierra Leonean Hip Hop fans may have placed on the incident. It also points to the aspirational nature of the local Hip Hop scene. The producers of the video wanted to show the significance of this rivalry, displaying an enthusiasm common among fans of American Rap when such beefs such as Biggie versus Tupac, or Jay-Z versus Nas, have arisen. LAJ finally gets his microphone back and finishes performing his song. In the rest of the video, we see the two artists trading off performances in an increasingly competitive tone. Akon, who eventually dons a Sierra Leonean flag, promises in the video to become "instrumental in making sure the world knows the talent that Sierra Leone has," and is clearly proud of his role as international African music ambassador. He seems oblivious to the onstage dynamics of his two in-vited guests. A few days after the concert, with rumours of tension building among Freetown youth, government ministers called Kao and LAJ in to settle their tensions. The two sheepishly acquiesced (Salone Jamboree 2010b), but the beef between their respective crews would persist throughout the following year.

Whatever the particular reasons for beef in the Sierra Leonean Rap scene (jealousy, greed, desire to make a name), beef has been common in Hip Hop since its New York beginnings in the 1970s. Journalist Algassimu Monoma Bah's history of Sierra Leonean Rap in the newspaper *Sierra Express Media* shows that beef between artists has always been a part of the local scene as well. As in New York, Hip Hop in Freetown started out as an underground phenomenon and lo-cal rappers would organise friendly battles to find out who was the most skilled lyricist. When the music began to enter the commercial market, Kao Denero and Pupa Bajah played out their rivalry through recorded songs. After Bajah left the country to concentrate on an international career, the door was open for Kao to take centre stage (Bah 2010). Today, as the self-proclaimed "King of Freetown," Kao Denero has become the main target for up-and-coming rappers. Kao himself blames jealousy as being at the root of the persistent beef, and has even tapped into common spiritual beliefs about jealousy's ability to cause harm through witchcraft after a hotel he was staying in burnt down (Salone Jamboree 2010c). Kao Denero and LAJ eventually broke their truce when Kao beat out LAJ for the Best Rapper award at the 2010 diaspora-based Sierra Leone Music Television Awards (Salone Jamboree 2010a). With both artists based in the US, the tension was left to simmer online and through local media platforms (Salone Jamboree 2010d), but residual effects from the rivalry would eventually be felt in Freetown.

On 11 and 12 December 2010, there was a series of rallies in Freetown held by several of the crews associated with leading Rappers in the country. These rallies were followed by two street skirmishes described as a riot in local media. On 13 December, 78 people appeared in court on charges ranging from riotous conduct to possession of offensive weapons. An association between supporters of rival Rap groups and rioters arose implicating the Dry Yai Crew, the West Africa Movement and the Red Flag Movement. The local newspaper, *Awareness Times*, reports:

> The rioters used the rallies of local musicians as opportunities to throw stones and other dangerous missiles, snatch mobile phones and valuable properties from peaceful residents ... [T]he police succeeded in arresting the aforementioned rioters following the launch of a rapid response operation using the anti riot team ... to coil down the deadly riots of Saturday and Sunday. Assistant Superintendent of Police (ASP) Ibrahim Samura used the forum as an opportunity to call on members of the public to help the police to weed out these misguided youths from society. He assured Sierra Leoneans that the police is on top of national security situation and there is no cause for panic. (Samba 2010)

As the above excerpt shows, youth violence in any form is enough to sound an alarm on the streets of Freetown. Especially telling is the reference to the incident in terms of "national security." This language highlights the real fear of youth violence that remains in the public consciousness after the war. In this specific set of events, it seems that the "various cult and gangster clubs (cliques)" that carried out the violence aligned themselves with different Rap crews, and started using the rallies to settle scores (Kabia 2010). Although channelled through what initially looks like an American-influenced practice, such incidents have long been part of the social landscape in Freetown.

Even though the Rappers were cleared of the charges of violence, a ban on musical shows remained throughout the holiday season that year. While the government's attempt to control the activities of popular musicians and their fans was most likely an attempt to bolster the appearance of its control over the social order, some members of the public opined that this was a strategy to deflect attention from the politicians' complicity in continued violence. Bah's article published in the *Sierra Express Media* a few days after the event illustrates this view:

> Instead of threatening to ban shows and rallies, find a way to help these artists move to the next level. Other than inviting artists like Akon and paying them hundreds of thousands of dollars, stick to these local artists and pay them that money. Show them they have value and promote them internationally ... [F]or the youths running around with gang violence, government has the obligation to create jobs and take them off the streets and not just rein in and blame them

when there is a problem. Politicians use these same young people during elections to cause havoc, what do you think you will get back? (2010)

Bah makes a good point about the need to engage youth on a deeper level, but transferring the blame from musicians to politicians misses the meaning inherent in the violence perpetrated by youth in Sierra Leone. The youth are aware of the power that violence conveys in the society at large, and since the war they've been aware of the implications of employing it. Their attraction to a violent cultural aesthetic and participation in actual violence is part of a political project that extends back before the war and is informed by modes of social navigation as well as a desire to be recognised as equal members of local and global society. While local media in Freetown are familiar with young people's cultural production, they fail to recognise youth violence as a project in the service of claims to youth's right to be political speakers in a complex system of formal and informal governance.

Colonial Dialectics

Political speech acts in any context can be better understood by analysing the formation of the social structures that inform them. In contemporary Sierra Leone, violence and various forms of cultural production are the principal vehicles through which an emancipatory politics is played out. To neutralise these emancipatory claims made by marginalised sections of the society, the regime seeks to absorb these elements into their various policing apparatuses. In doing this, the ruling elite seeks to control who has the right to be a political speaker, what qualifies as political speech and when political speech can happen. The current consensus form of democracy in Sierra Leone is marked by a hierarchical social order in which qualifications for political speech are determined by membership in, or connection to a class of professional politicians. This state structure has roots in the colonial era when the British instituted two separate governance systems: an urban colony on the Freetown peninsula and a separate native administration run through indirect rule in the protectorate. Let us now look briefly at Sierra Leone's political history to further understand how current forms of political speech came about.

Throughout Sierra Leone's history, various subordinated populations were able to engage in their own brand of dissent politics against the dominant order. The residents of the Upper Guinea Coast moulded implicit forms of protest and self-preservation during the long and violent history of the transatlantic slave trade. These modes of social navigation helped shape cultural practices and beliefs throughout Sierra Leonean history (Shaw 1997, 2001, Ferme 2001). Towards the end of the slave trade, the British laid the foundations for the modern state of Sierra Leone when they established the Freetown Colony as a safe haven for former slaves from around the Atlantic region. Within the confines of the colony, British social norms and governing policies were dominant. Africans living in this space had to dispute the notions of what belonged to and was proper to urban colonial society. The repatriated settlers on the Freetown peninsula had ancestral origins all over West and Central Africa, and were returning to the continent with cultures moulded in the Americas from Brazil to Canada. A new ethnic identity emerged that blended Western customs with pan-African ones, creating the Krios. Even though the British retained administrative control over Freetown, the hybrid Krio culture soon came to dominate local society. This new culture partially birthed the idea of an African-British citizen, and would ultimately benefit the British by solidifying their hold on their small Western outpost on a yet to be colonised continent.

Throughout the colonial era, Krios sat firmly between the Europeans and the hinterland Africans, wavering in their cultural and political loyalties between both groups. In the administration of the colony, the Krios became the civil servant intermediaries that would uphold the normal order prescribed by the British, but also fight their logic of domination through claims of the equality of Africans. At times, violent dissent would arise, most prominently during the Hut Tax War of 1898 when the British tried to establish control over the protectorate, and in later colonial years through the radical labour organising of Wallace-Johnson (Abdullah 1998). Since the British had a general monopoly on violence, violence was a rarer form of political contestation. Instead, dissent against British domination took the form of cultural practices that carved out space for the new identities developing in the local social milieu. Freetown's Krios incorporated pan-African and Western elements into local culture, creating new hybrid forms, and were able to assert claims to belonging in the urban social fabric (Stasik 2011: 34).

The merging of African and Western modes of social organisation, which first appeared as a form of political contestation about belonging in colonial society, quickly became the foundation for the normal order of urban life in the capital. In the wake of the migration of people from the indigenous provinces to Freetown, the Krios would lose a numerical majority, and eventually their political and economic dominance in the capital. Culturally, the Krios remained influential. Their cultural hybridity, language and worldviews served as the main pathway for assimilation into a globally oriented urban society. Those migrating from the interior would form their own urban societies as a means of both self- and community-empowerment (Nunley 1985, Stasik 2011: 39–41).

A plethora of unique forms of artistic expression arose in Freetown's cultural landscape. One of the more influential groups in Freetown was the fairly large Yoruba population. It was this community that served as a cultural wellspring for the *ode-lay* societies, street carnival masquerades organised around African spiritual beliefs. These urban societies not only served as places for African populations to form a unique cultural identity, but also provided systems of support and social navigation alternative to the norms set out by the British (Nunley 1988). Also developing during the colonial era were the hybrid Islamic-secular Lantern Parades in Freetown. Allegedly borrowed from The Gambia, these parades of hand-crafted lanterns and floats resembled the carnival processions of the Caribbean. Thus, they became one of the many cultural elements in Freetown that helped provide continuity in transoceanic cultural dialogues (Nunley 1985). Both the *ode-lays* and Lantern Parades allowed for the establishment of a professional class of artists in Freetown, and served as nodes for local communities and neighbourhoods to organise around (Nunley 1985). Music was also a central part of these traditions. Bobo Music, Goombay, Palm Wine and Mailo Jazz were separate musical genres forged in colonial Freetown that borrowed influences from around the Atlantic world (Nunley 1985, Nunley 1988, Stasik 2011: 37). Through these forms of expression, birthed in a culturally diverse urban environment, the Sierra Leone colony came to occupy a key space of cultural formation, exchange and influence in the greater Atlantic world.

While dissent politics were present during the colonial period, they did not play as much of a role during Sierra Leone's transition to independence. African claims to citizenship and belonging in the urban context had been reasonably recognised through cultural contestations initiated by the Krios. While a radical politics did start in the late colonial period through the Wallace-Johnson-led labour movement, his subsequent jailing and exile closed the formal pathways for radical politics at the national level. When Sierra Leone was granted statehood in 1962, the revolutionary politics apparent in other parts of West Africa remained largely absent (Abdullah 1998).

Further shaping the Sierra Leone postcolonial order was the political marginalisation of the Krios. Instead of handing control of the new state to the group that had helped maintain the colonial order for so many years, British authorities handed power to Western-educated upper- and middle-class professionals from ruling families in the indigenous interior. With these newly appointed leaders in place, the nation's formation was negotiated peacefully through the creation of a consensus democracy. Building on the foundation set during British rule, the rulers of the new country fused a Western-modelled democracy with the protectorate's system of rural governance. The protectorate had been run by the British native administration through a system of indirect rule. This system was enforced by paramount chiefs appointed by the colonial government to carry out tax collection, and one's citizenship and access to state resources was defined by one's proximity to these figures (Fanthorpe 2001). The incorporation of these modes of governance into the independent state would allow future presidents to engineer a neopatrimonial one-party system.

The cultural hybridity that was the main form of political dissent during the colonial era, became the foundation for the normal order after independence, exemplifying what Rancière calls the "vanishing point" of politics. However, as Rancière argues, once old subjectivities are accepted as part of the normal order, new subjectivities will enter the field of perception to make claims as political speakers (Corcoran 2010). In Sierra Leone, these new subjectivities ultimately came from politically and economically marginalised populations in both the rural and urban areas. It was these subjectivities that would lead to the violent uprising that became the civil war.

Policing Informal Networks

Today, in the wake of a failure of the neopatrimonial state, the dichotomy between Africa and the West and its accompanying notion of the proper has returned with a vengeance. Under the influence of thinkers such as Robert Kaplan, liberal democracy and open market capitalism have become the norms prescribed for social order by the international community. The failure of the Sierra Leonean government to uphold this order during the war years was part of the initial reasoning behind the New Barbarism thesis. In the postwar years, the installation of an internationally sponsored liberal peace-building project, accompanied by such projects as the Truth and Reconciliation Commission and the Sierra Leone Special Court, has forced the Sierra Leonean state to conform to these global perceptions of the normal order. The familiar phenomenon of imposing order from the outside is accompanied by a latent, somewhat hypocritical belief among the international community that Africans are unable to do so themselves. At the same time, local informal networks have forced politicians to recreate a hybrid form of governance, just as had happened during the post-independence period. In the place of a neopatrimonialism based on colonial indirect rule, what has emerged today is a hybrid democracy that incorporates formal modes of governance combined with informal networks informed by local notions of social navigation and order (Taylor 2009, Utas 2012). The modes of policing that have arisen in Sierra Leone are often employed through both formal and informal channels simultaneously.

Given the lack of a state-supported safety net, informal social networks in Sierra Leone assume central importance in an average person's daily life. There are many different informal networks one individual can belong to or access. Kinship, for instance, remains an important tool for social navigation. It is no secret that one way to get things done in Sierra Leone is to have a relative working in or connected to the government take care of it for you. While visiting Freetown in 2011, I was encouraged to secure everything from a deal in the market to a passport by playing on familial ties. Pass by any ministry, and you can see lines of people waiting their turn for an audience with a certain minister, who is expected to solve the personal problem regardless of his or her official state function. For good or bad, these modes of social navigation help shape the normal order of life. Perhaps this is not unique to Sierra Leone, or even Africa (Utas 2012).

Another informal network, ethnic identity, had a somewhat sinister character on the streets of Freetown in 2011. Ethnic tension is one of the social problems most often associated with African conflict, and its persistence in global conflict is a central tenet of the New Barbarism thesis. However, ethnic tension was never considered a direct cause of Sierra Leone's civil war, so it surprised me to find that in the wake of the 2007 elections ethnic identity had been increasingly incorporated into party politics. The extent to which it had penetrated daily life became evident one night after I had visited a nightclub in the West End of Freetown.

It was early in the morning when I took a *Poda Poda* bus ride from the club area in Lumley beach to the Eastern police station on the edge of downtown. On the bus, people began a lively conversation about who would become the flag bearer for the Sierra Leone People's Party (SLPP) at the political convention happening that day. Two young men became engaged in a very heated exchange. As one young man was getting out of the vehicle, he told the other he didn't know what he was talking about, while the other shouted back, "You look like a Mende man." Several people told me this phrase had become a common insult in postwar Temne-dominated Freetown, aimed at those critical of the ruling All People's Congress (APC). This insult may be used even where the person insulted does not even belong to the Mende ethnic group. This is an interesting conflation of physical appearance and political alignment, meant to show one no longer has individual political agency, but is rather a tribally aligned party loyalist. While I was amazed at the level of engagement with mainstream politics among post-club revellers early in the morning, I was even more surprised that ethnic identity and its associated tensions had reared its head so casually, and in such a public location.

Examining the modes of political navigation employed by politicians can help us better sort out the meaning of ethnic identity in *Sierra Leonean* politics. In anthropologist Michael Jackson's book In Sierra Leone, we see one of Sierra Leone's longest serving career politicians, S.B. Marah, navigate between his job and his ethnic loyalties. In Jackson's account, Marah holds on to his ethnic identity in his governmental dealings because he perceives that the Western-modelled state has not always worked for Sierra Leone: "When S.B. invoked Kuranko-ness, it was not some form of tribalism that he had in mind, but the values he held dear – not only forthrightness, stoicism, hard work, and self-reliance, but also honesty, generosity, and fidelity to one's principles" (Jackson 2004: 99). In a nation where state institutions have not proven powerful enough to enforce social order, some see dependency on values informed by tradition as a necessary mode of operation.

Yet in at least one instance, we see Marah clearly reject the incorporation of tribal identity into party politics. The anecdote Marah relates begins with a group of Kuranko men, the northern ethnic group he belongs to, coming to retrieve him from an SLPP meeting so that he can attend a meeting of their tribal *ferensola* organisation. After he refused to join them, they reported to the local chief that S.B. had abandoned his tribal affiliation and gone over to the Mendes. Marah explains: "They called a meeting of chiefs in Kabala, and I was chastised for having left *ferensola* ... I explained to the few I met that *ferensola* was neither APC [n]or SLPP. One could be both an APC member and part of *ferensola*, or an SLPP member and part of *ferensola*" (Jackson 2004: 167). This account shows that Marah was aware of the line between his duty to the nation and to his ethnic group. It also highlights the balance of obligations that a Sierra Leone politician must achieve, as well as the real repercussions the perception of ethnic loyalty can have (Adolfo 2010).

Sierra Leone is far from being a completely ethnic- or kinship-aligned society. As Jackson notes, personal relationships such as long friendships within peer groups, connections made through school, and in-laws are just as likely to lead to political connections and to promote loyalties to certain individuals or parties (Jackson 2004: 214). This is definitely true in the current political system, where perhaps the most significant informal networks are those constructed during wartime across ethnic, regional or religious lines (Peters 2007, Hoffman 2007, Utas 2012). Additionally, according to Richard Fanthorpe, social allegiances in rural Sierra Leone have been historically fluid. It wasn't until the British set up their system of indirect rule through taxation by local chiefs that ethnicity and kinship became more important forms of social identification. It was the fundamental British misunderstanding of the way rural society functioned that helped harden these networks (Fanthorpe 2001). Today, there is a multitude of informal networks in the country, and Sierra Leoneans of all backgrounds employ them to their advantage in a host of situations.

What quickly became clear in the run-up to the elections of 2012 is that a renewed ethnic and regional tension in party politics has become an informal tool that is exploited by politicians to secure or gain power in formal institutions. In the internationally monitored postwar period, it is elections that dictate the transfer of power between political parties. By relying on ethnic identity in a country evenly split between Temne- and Mende-aligned regions, politicians can manipulate a strong informal network to influence the vote.

The desire for political control has always been a major motive in the manipulation of informal networks, such as ethnic affiliation in Sierra Leone. The relationship between ethnicity and formal institutions stretches back to the early years of independence, when former President Albert Margai staffed the upper echelons of his army with tribal loyalists. This strategy helped lead to a coup in 1967, which sought to return him to power. More recently, former President Tejan Kabbah was criticised for depending too much on ethnic affiliation in fighting off rebels during the civil war. In 1997, Kabbah was ousted in a military coup by the Armed Forces Revolutionary Council (AFRC). Upon his return to power, he disbanded the army and relied on Mende-aligned *Kamajors*, as well as foreign forces (Adolfo 2010). His mistrust of the army and the breakdown of the formal armed forces led Kabbah to depend on ethnic allegiance as a stronger social bond. Today, the consolidation of power by manipulating ethnic identity continues, adapting itself to party campaigning in mainstream politics.

The hybrid formal-informal nature of social and political organisation does not always make it easy to identify the modes of social navigation employed by both politicians and citizens in Sierra Leone. Many outside observers remain mystified by the local social order and are blinded by their own perceptions of what is proper to the realm of politics. Jackson sees how Marah is received in his homeland and notes that it made him "aware of how spurious it was to try and distinguish between chieftaincy and political power in S.B.'s case. Indeed, in Kuranko, one is commonly assimilated to the other, political office being known as the white man's chieftaincy" (2004: 16). Another outside observer, Ian Taylor, identifies a hybrid neopatrimonial state based on traditional social structures in Sierra Leone. He discusses how a formal Western liberal democratic bureaucracy works as a cover for an informal system of political clientelism. Taylor one of those who suggests that the formation of a state that conforms to Western conceptions has failed, and that Sierra Leone lacks the foundations for a rational, bureaucratic, liberal, democratic state. He argues that even in the postwar period, Sierra Leone is a textbook example of a neopatrimonial state in displaying four characteristics: clientelism, privileged access to state resources, centralisation of power, and a hybrid regime that retains the appearance of a rational-bureaucratic state, but which elites are able to manipulate to their own advantage. This translates into a daily balancing act in which government needs "to maintain a degree of political stability [for international donors] by satisfying the regime's supporters and weakening its opponents" (Taylor 2009). Here Taylor is identifying Sierra Leonean politicians' twin modes of consolidating power and maintaining the established order. These dual modes of policing, the elimination of competition and the privileging of supporters, are the main forms of informal social control employed by political elites in the country.

Yet, this criticism of Sierra Leone's political environment misses key elements in the informal political system. Taylor and other outside observers fail to recognise the forms of political navigation that are in fact democratic and available to all parts of the population. The hybrid nature of Sierra Leonean society illustrates that Western and African norms of social navigation are not incompatible or even mutually exclusive. The logic of the cultural other that underpins a dichotomy between Africa and the West is false. Cultural hybridity has been part of the normal social order since Europeans first arrived on Sierra Leonean shores. There has been a constant interplay and exchange between the two, with European cultural practices shaping African ones and vice versa. Today in Sierra Leone, individuals from all social backgrounds use both informal and formal networks to navigate their daily lives. So it is through both formal and informal social structures that marginalised individuals and social groups are able to contest their place in society. The forms of speech that result are the modes of political contestation that shape what belongs to the realm of the proper. Importantly, contrary to what some international observers may believe, even though Sierra Leonean social organisation retains informal characteristics, this does not mean that the forms of political participation in that system are undemocratic. In fact, the forms of political speech that arise are much more in line with Rancière's ideas of democracy than the consensus forms of prescribed by international donors.

As we have seen, during the early stages of hinterland colonisation, formerly fluid traditional social structures were inscribed in hard form into the system of indirect colonial rule. In turn, the rural social structures solidified during this period helped shape the postcolonial state by creating a hybrid system of formal and informal governance. Traditional belief is that power in society flows down from ancestors to elders and finally to youth (Ellis 2007). This belief was co-opted by the British to enforce their top-down rule over the colonial hinterland. When the British relinquished Sierra Leone, the system of domination of Europeans over Africans morphed into a state system in which elders dominated youth. The marginal status of young people in contemporary West Africa is often framed through this cultural lens (Saucier 2011: 51–68). From the standpoint of political dissensus, *elders* corresponds with the ruling elite recognised as those fit to rule, and *youth* with the marginalised masses considered unqualified for political speech (Hoffman 2006). Political parties in contemporary Sierra Leone retain this organising structure, with elders at the top, and legions of conscripted youth carrying out their orders at the bottom. When one party takes power, large numbers of Sierra Leoneans remain excluded from political participation, and even those conscripted into the ranks of the political party are beholden to the party leaders (Christensen and Utas 2008). As a result, dissensus in Sierra Leone exists where marginalised populations struggle to qualify as political speakers in a realm where elders rule.

To better understand the elder-youth dynamic played out through political party hierarchies, it is important to recognise that in West Africa youth is a category not contained by biological age (Christiansen, Utas *et al.* 2006). This distinction is integral to understanding the political identity of youth, and can help us understand how various forms of dissent politics came into existence throughout Sierra Leonean history. Importantly, not all young people must be of the youth, and not all youth are necessarily young. The way in which Mats Utas and Maya Christensen use the term is how I will use it throughout this paper:

> As is obvious in current writings on Africa, "youth" is a highly context-dependent and fluid signifier. But the way we use it in this text, which we think reflects the way it is generally used in West Africa, is as a label for marginalized young (and not so young) people, rather than for a whole population within a certain age bracket. The potential danger of youth is thus not dependent on bulging demographic processes, as popularly supposed, but rather on the number of young people experiencing socio-economic marginalization and powerlessness. (2008: 517)

The nature of the term "youth" in Sierra Leone is underscored by the way Sierra Leoneans imagine social mobility. To move from youth to elder, one must first be able to start a family. Lack of economic means limits one's ability to marry and raise children. This means that economics, adulthood and social status are intimately intertwined, and economically marginalised individuals can become stuck in perpetually delayed adulthood (Shepler 2008, Stasik 2011: 148). As Sierra Leonean singer Sorie Kondi puts it: "Without money, you nor get family."

Contributing to the formation of a collective youth political identity in Sierra Leone is the continued importance of informal networks. While social networks through kinship ties remain a means of social navigation for many Sierra Leoneans, urban youths are often disconnected from family networks in rural homelands. In their place, young people use informal urban networks as a social safety net: everything from trade unions such as the Cassette Seller's Association and the Okada (Bike) Rider's Association, urban societies like *ode-lay*, and the crews, gangs, and cliques that form around Gangsta Rap culture. Many of these networks are a continuation of those formed during the civil war among groups of combatants (Peters 2007). Once formed, these networks can turn a collective of marginalised individuals into significant political forces. Since social mobility is determined by access to financial resources, networks connected to power and wealth become all the more significant.

Thinking of youth as a marginalised political category can help clarify the forms of political contestation that take place in Sierra Leone. Jackson points out that in traditional rural society, such contestations served as an important check and balance on elders. When those in power do not behave in ways proper to their status, they may lose their titles. As ascribed social positions are not necessarily hard and fast, social boundaries can and should be contested from all directions. In some rural societies, whenever there was a social imbalance, a disruptive politics was believed to necessarily precede a return to social order (Jackson 2004: 47). Since youth is an ascribed social position, initiation rituals, the traditional site of mobility into adulthood, become important symbols of political contestation. Often in initiation rituals, a violent rupture between youth and adulthood is connoted. One example is that during initiation a child may be *eaten* by the bush, die and then re-emerge anew in adult form. This may provide insight into the deeper connections between violence, ritual and rebellion in West Africa in general (Ellis 2007, Moran 2008, Utas 2008).

Because of the dialectical nature of dissensus, there will never be an end to politics, but that doesn't mean violence as a vehicle for dissent cannot be supplanted by another form of political speech. The arts appear in Sierra Leonean history as a form of public dissent in precolonial society, as well throughout colonialism. Youth would engage in political contestation in the form of masquerades, plays, songs and murals (Nunley 1982, 1985, 1988, Opala 1994, Christensen and Utas 2008, Shepler 2010). There were many examples of youth political contestation during Sierra Leone's recent history, so a brief review of the various forms of such contestation immediately prior to, during and after the civil war is warranted.

Rarrays, Rebels and Rappers

The violent rebellion of the Sierra Leone civil war, described as a crisis of youth by many observers, had its origin in the formation of an oppositional youth identity organised around popular culture during the Siaka Stevens dictatorship of the 1970s. At this time, a new identity, *rarray boys*, took shape among marginalised urban youth, a group Ibrahim Abdullah refers to as Sierra Leone's *lumpenproletariat*. The creation of this identity was facilitated by the *pote*, a hang-out where street youth would get together, smoke marijuana, listen to revolutionary music and discuss pan-African politics. Figures such as Bob Marley, Kwame Nkrumah, Wallace-Johnson and Marcus Garvey played a prominent role in their discourse (1998). Also important were the *ode-lays*, also known as devil societies, who often ran their own *potes*. The term *devil* as the central figure in the *ode-lay* masquerades was coined by missionaries in Freetown, who were turned off by the non-Christian spirituality inherent in the practice. So, during colonial times these figures were already cast to the margins of civilised urban society. With Sierra Leonean independence, *ode-lays* were more accepted in mainstream society as an institution of national heritage. Public and official opinion on *ode-lays* alternated between cultural pride and nuisance, as civil disruption and fierceness were key parts of their masquerading practices. These opinions were reflected in and influenced by the state-controlled press, which derided or praised different *ode-lay* groups at their convenience (Nunley 1982). For marginalised urban street youths, *ode-lays* and *potes* were attractive places to express a rebellious identity and incubate ideas of opposition to mainstream politics. These revolutionary ideas also spread to middle-class students at Forah Bay College. The energy of this new informal oppositional youth culture propelled a politics of rebellion, and led to protests and a strike in 1977 organised by student leaders. This was the first time since independence that young people had intervened in the political arena around a clear agenda of political reform (Abdullah 1998: 210). Because of the structure of power in Sierra Leone, these claims to the recognition of political speech by youth were extremely disruptive of the normal social order. Stevens eventually clamped down on political dissent, demobilising and suppressing the student movement through violence and other modes of policing.

Lining up opposite the emerging political youth identity was the practice of incorporating youth into the political party machine. This was one of the most effective modes of policing employed by the Stevens regime. As a means of social mobility, *rarray boys* joined the ranks of the political party, and were armed and organised into enforcement forces. They were then sent out to use violence and enforce order as dictated from above. As regards cultural production, *ode-lay* groups would gain favour with the regime by supporting the party during their masquerades. Wealthy individuals and influential politicians would sponsor an *ode-lay* group to perform masquerades in their honour (Nunley 1988). Just as with ethnicity, youth violence was often used to hold on to power and enforce order.

The trade-off between youth as oppositional political identity and youth incorporation into the policing regime was mirrored in the popular music audiences of the 1970s. As mentioned before, Reggae music became a polarising force around revolutionary ideas (Abdullah 1998), and music played a central role in the success of *ode-lay* masquerades (Nunley 1988). However, even with a high potential to have a political impact on the youth, Afro National and Super Combo, the two most popular bands in Freetown at this time, remained markedly apolitical in their content. The impact of these bands was such that their large fan bases developed a passionate rivalry, splitting the city in two. As Stasik notes "respective rival fan groups' composition crossed all ... social, economic, ethnic, religious, and political lines" (2011: 49). The choice of which band to support was arbitrary, likened by one of Stasik's informants to the rivalry between football teams. In a sense, musical fandom appears at this time as a strong informal social network able to draw people together across social boundaries, and perhaps even provide a means of social navigation and support.

The potential importance of these networks for daily navigation in Freetown raises questions about the true political meaning behind this rivalry. Stasik speculates about why such a rivalry would take shape at a time of harsh political oppression. He surmises there may have been patron-client relationships between bands and members of Freetown's elite, mirroring a practice common to *ode-lays* and to musicians throughout various eras in Sierra Leone's history. This rivalry could have served as a distraction from the politics of repression the state was engaging in: the masses had to be kept happy to avoid some sort of revolt. Stasik calls this a "bread and circuses" approach to social control (2011: 49). So, while music at this time was very much used as a social unifier in oppositional politics, it was also possible for music to be incorporated into modes of policing. What is most interesting for our purposes is the precedent this rivalry set for the Gangster Rap rivalries that grip Freetown's youth populations today.

After the slow disintegration of APC's one-party state, a military coup led by young soldiers was welcomed as a youth-led revolution in 1992. The tipping point for the military was the government's incompetence in handling the Revolutionary United Front (RUF) invasion into eastern Sierra Leone. This coup was especially celebrated by young people, many of whom were influenced by the same pan-African and radical politics, music and aesthetics that influenced the previous generation. Youth took to the streets and painted revolutionary murals celebrating the coup's leaders and the possibilities of a new future for Sierra Leone (Opala 1994). Unfortunately, the RUF rebellion continued in the countryside, and youth came to play a prominent fighting role in the civil war that soon engulfed the country. In addition, an associated youth culture informed by American Hip Hop, especially Gangsta Rap, came to reflect the rebel soldiers' worldview. These soldiers adapted Gangsta Rap aesthetics to wartime, and used it as a military tactic to instil fear in the civilian population (Utas and Jörgel 2008). The appropriation of Tupac was most explicit during the formation of the splinter AFRC (Armed Force's Revolutionary Council) faction of the West Side Boys, who would go on a countrywide raid from their exile in eastern Sierra Leone back to Freetown. Once they arrived in Freetown, Tupac and his accompanying Gangsta Rap aesthetics would figure prominently in people's minds as the young soldiers unleashed horror on the civilian population. Even with this history, Tupac would be adapted to the immediate postwar context and appropriated as a symbol of peace and reconciliation by appearing on T-shirts alongside his rival Rapper Notorious B.I.G. (Prestholdt 2009: 214). The adaptability of Tupac's music and images to such opposing contexts illustrates an important fluidity in the meaning of music and of youth political participation in Sierra Leone.

During the waning years of the war, there was boom in local music production, and local artists became highly popular among local audiences. This boom was initiated in 1999 when Jimmy Bangura, popularly known as Jimmy B, returned to Sierra Leone after a life spent travelling and making music in the US, England and South Africa. By bringing in technical skills and encouraging youth to rap in local languages to beats that encompassed a mix of dance styles from around the Black Atlantic, he singlehandedly birthed Sierra Leone's postwar youth music revolution (Panton 2006). In Freetown, a new urban cultural identity grew up and supplanted the youth culture formed in violent rebellion. Jimmy B's efforts were supported by various NGOs that were keen to engage former combatants in the demobilisation and reintegration process. These NGOs put on events and concerts all over the country, and provided an outlet for cultural production by many of the youth that had been engaged in violent rebellion. The influx of foreign workers and money greatly affected the political economy of Sierra Leone. The local night life industry was boosted as workers sought out entertainment options in their downtime. New nightclubs mushroomed around Freetown, and foreign entities provided opportunities for the social advancement of youth that circumvented traditional social hierarchies. The postwar period was marked by celebration, national pride and the marking of a new era. Aided by the mandates of international NGOs and the money of foreign workers, locally produced music themes reflected this optimism (Stasik 2011: 65).

After this optimistic immediate postwar period, many of the youth started

to become disillusioned with the political and economic situation in the country. It seemed that the SLPP would be unable to address promptly the problems
of poverty and corruption that had existed before the civil war. Artists such as
The Jungle Leaders, Emmerson and Daddy Saj sang oppositional songs that
railed against corrupt elders sitting in the government offices. The youth culture
coalescing around the local music scene quickly became engaged with an oppositional politics. By the time of the elections of 2007, the role of music in the
political realm was firmly established. This election was seen as a watershed moment in Sierra Leone's fragile democracy. As Utas and Christensen note, "The
first general election since the UN [withdrawal of] the majority of its peacekeeping forces, it was a key event for both the nation and for international donors"
(2008: 518). Channelling the frustrations of a majority of Sierra Leoneans, musicians became popular by singing songs criticising the ruling administration
and political elders in general. Shepler identifies three main categories of political music during this time: music about political parties and candidates, music
that was explicitly political but rejected an association with political parties, and
implicitly political social commentaries in music. If one could draw a line from
the urban oppositional youth culture that emerged in the 1970s to the rebellious
youth war of the 1990s, one could also draw a line from youth participation in
a violent rebellion to youth participation in the political music leading up to the
election of 2007 (Abdullah 2007, Shepler 2010).

Violence was not totally absent during those elections. Just as with the Siaka
Stevens regime of the 1970s, violence was incorporated into the policing apparatus by way of marginalised youth populations. The lead candidates from
both parties acknowledged the potential for political violence inherent in the
existence of mass youth unemployment. In the context of growing public disillusionment, instead of allowing for the return of a rebellious politics of violence,
political parties incorporated youth into their ranks. Party leaders let the youth
believe that if their party won, youth would be rewarded. This time, instead
of youth leagues, the conscripted youth were known as *task forces*. Instead of
lumpenproletariat, they were called *ex-combatants* (Christensen and Utas 2008).
Politicians bribed former commanders from rebel factions to conscript their
erstwhile soldiers into the ranks of the political party. These youths were then
officially employed as political party members. Often, rival rebel groups were
aligned opposite their former rivals in an opposing political party. In a strange
replay of wartime battlefield dynamics, AFRC's West Side Boys aligned with
SLPP and the RUF with APC. Fearing for their own safety, many youths saw
no other option to joining the ranks of political parties. The violence came to a
climax on 1 September 2007, when rival members of the APC and SLPP clashed
in the streets of Freetown in the run-up to the second round of elections (Christensen and Utas 2008).

Even though many youths participated in the campaigning, they still recognised the futility of believing the current system of consensus democracy would lead to fundamental change in their daily lives. One youth equated the form of democracy that was being played out to supporting a football team: "I know nothing about politics, I really don't care about politics ... it is just a game. It is just like football. The government of today is the government of tomorrow" (Christensen and Utas 2008: 530). This equating of the two parties with a football team echoes the sentiments expressed by followers of Super Combo and Afro National during the 1970s. Continued support of a party while pretending to support another became known as *Watermelon Politics* (Abdullah 2007, Utas 2007). This was a social navigation strategy that individuals and small groups employed to manipulate the formal system of consensus democracy for individual gain. It was so named after the practice of someone purporting to support the SLPP, whose colours were green, and then turning around and voting for the red APC, or vice versa. Some youths were bold enough to work as campaigners for both parties at the same time, on the same day. This was dangerous, because anyone found out was dealt with harshly. Another *Watermelon Politics* tactic was to use one's violent reputation as a means of extortion, regardless of party affiliation. Notorious former combatants would exact money from prominent and wealthy politicians by using the threat of violence, sometimes donning the opposite party's colours as a guise (Christensen and Utas 2008). While they may not immediately appear so, these modes of participation in the policing regime were a means of dissent. By playing the game of party politics for individual social gain, youth were able to delegitimise the power politicians held over them.

Reflecting the ability and desire of politicians to co-opt political violence in their favour, music was also incorporated into the system of political campaigning. The songs openly critical of the ruling party were easily co-opted by the opposition, but when artists were critical of the ruling party, it wasn't always easy to tell if they were being so in direct support of the opposition or not. Connections between artists and politicians were rarely made public, as audiences preferred artists seen as authentic voices of dissent:

> In all of these songs (and other similar ones), the singers speak from the position of "youth man den" (young men). However, it is not necessarily easy to speak for the "youth man den". There is some popular derision for government or NGO-sponsored songs (e.g. USAID-funded songs about AIDS prevention). Songs lose their power if they are too clearly speaking on behalf [of] some party, and therefore elders, and not on behalf of the interests of the youth. (Shepler 2010: 636)

Rumours arose that certain artists were paid off, and "dubious figures, supposedly political backers, roamed about the streets of Freetown, distributing free copies of the songs among the people, and 'dashing' bus and taxi drivers to play them during their rides" (Stasik 2011: 69). It quickly became evident that musicians had become fully incorporated into the electioneering machine. As Stasik, Utas and Christensen note, politicians had no qualms about making it seem that collaboration would provide future opportunities. While this inducement was mostly taken with a grain of salt, as evidenced by such phenomena as *Watermelon Politics*, the modes of policing through co-option of political music eventually helped destroy the credibility of local political music.

The ability of politicians to manipulate musical output in their favour, regardless of the artist's intentions, can be clearly illustrated by the case of Emmerson Bockarie. Before the election of 2007, one of the biggest tunes in the country was Emmerson's hit "Borbor Bele." The song was championed by the opposition APC as a critique of the ruling SLPP. Emmerson shot to stardom as Sierra Leone's number one revolutionary artist. After the APC won the 2007 election, many people credited the musician, and others like him, with helping to usher in a new era of democracy in Sierra Leone. At first, musicians paused their critiques waiting to see if the new administration would usher in change. After two years, Emmerson felt that the APC, too comfortable with its popularity, was not acting as they had promised, so he spoke up. He released a song called "Yesterday Better Pass Tiday," meaning yesterday was better than today. Emmerson's criticism of the government was not as welcome this time around. Many thought he had been co-opted by the SLPP, thus destroying his credibility as a political voice of the people. Not long after the release of "Yesterday Better Pass Today," a Rapper named Innocent, whose "Injectment Notice" was one of the more influential tunes during the ousting of the SLPP, came out with his own song called "Una Gi Dem Chance." He insulted Emmerson, and asked Sierra Leoneans to give the APC time to prove its worth. Innocent was asked by the government to perform his song at the opening of a long-awaited hydroelectric dam project. It started to become clear that Innocent was a tool of the APC (Kraft 2010). This new music rivalry, more explicitly political than that between Afro National and Super Combo, began to resemble the policing strategy of weakening opponents and privileging supporters (Taylor 2009). Even though the APC had used Emmerson's music for its own ends during the election, after he turned against the party it tried to neutralise his power as a political speaker by painting him as a tribalist and SLPP loyalist. It is perhaps evident that APC's cries of corruption were masking many politicians' own desires to have their turn at the font of state-connected resources. The perceived divisions between political parties served as a mask for the real divisions in the country.

The elections of 2007 were deemed successful by the international community, and the peacekeeping and democracy-building organisations completed their pull out. With them went much of the material support for local musicians and the booming local industry. In the end, the integration of the local music industry into the liberal peace-building project may have been a central factor contributing to the downturn in local production after the elections. After visiting Sierra Leone in the summer of 2011, it became evident to me that the international community's withdrawal had led to an economic recession in the country, affecting everyone from informal petty traders to real estate agents. On the streets of Freetown, people generally felt that when the West left the country, so went their money. This meant that economically and politically marginalised youths had again to fend for themselves in the face of an entrenched system of rule by political elders. Adding to the decline in the local music industry was the fact that Sierra Leonean music had become so associated with the politics of the consensus regime that once a "politics fatigue" swept the country, so did a fatigue with local music (Stasik 2011: 55, 122). The type of music Sierra Leonean audiences preferred suddenly shifted from locally engaged political music to foreign-produced output that was about the realm of the domestic and the personal. This new globally oriented musical aesthetic signalled the hopes and dreams of individuals to attain a new life reality at some future point. Stasik argues that this implied a move from music concerned with politics and the public realm, to a desire to consume music concerned with the social and the private realm. In contemporary Sierra Leone, it is this music that speaks to ideas of global and local belonging, and informs notions of social mobility for marginalised populations (2011: 149-55). However, one must be careful not to dislocate the content of the music from the political context within which it is being produced and consumed. As Rancière argues, politics always seeks to blur the lines between the social and the political, the private and the public, and what is proper to their respective realms (Corcoran 2010: 3). The choice to adapt specific cultural elements by marginalised groups can very much signal the continued contestation of accepted social norms.

In a video uploaded to Youtube by user Cathousemusiq named "Car shopping raaaaaaaaaa,"[4] we see LAJ standing in an antique car dealership somewhere in the US. The dreadlocked Rapper is wearing a red shirt with a white crucifix hung low around his neck. The dialogue starts with LAJ telling the camera operator he is interested in buying a classic car because he is tired of all the new models. The two shift between English, Krio and Hip Hop vernacular. A discussion of his spending habits ensues and he speculates about whether certain cars are within his budget. He stops at one car costing $22,000 and proudly claims it is within his price range. The conversation is dotted with various claims to the authenticity of the situation. He places the dealership in Michigan, and meets with an American car dealer. LAJ and the camera operator are performing claims to material wealth by way of an MTV cribs, commercial Hip Hop aesthetic. This is an attempt to represent a charmed American lifestyle. In a moment of promotion for an upcoming album, LAJ directly addresses all his fans back in Freetown, shouting out the names of different neighbourhoods in the city. We realise the desire to stage realness in this scene is meant for audiences who may never have been to or seen an American car dealership. For those familiar with the environment being represented, a wanting, aspirational nature of the video is evident.

As we have seen, international policy continues to be informed by narratives suggesting that during the war years Sierra Leone had fallen off the map of civilisation (cf., Ferguson 1999). This outlook still dominated in the postwar period, and as part of a liberal peace-building project the international community oversaw the installation of a consensus democratic regime and the country's integration into the global open-market economy. Today, the incentive to maintain the appearance of free and open elections remains high. Liberal democracy is a prerequisite for a state's membership in the new version of modernism known as globalisation, a membership necessary to access state-building resources from international bodies (Taylor 2009). As NGOs and state-based aid dwindles in Sierra Leone, the state increasingly needs to integrate into international networks of free-market trade. This is reflected by policies that concentrate on attracting foreign direct investment, principally through resource extraction industries, and international tourism. This has allowed Sierra Leone to become integrated into high-value networks of trade, and become the beneficiary of large infrastructure projects aimed at assisting international corporations, foreign governments and a global business elite. While economic analysts marvel at increases in the country's projected GDP, a majority of Sierra Leoneans remain

---

4. http://youtu.be/Bx84LrTL7qM

marginalised from such economic growth. The greater the country's integration into international business networks, the more Freetown resembles other global capitals as a splintered city. A globally connected political elite, business class and community of expats enjoy the fruits of economic development, isolated from a marginalised majority who remain cut off from basic public services and infrastructure enhancements (Graham and Marvin 2006).

While the splintered city is defined by a divide in access to physical infrastructure, the fluidity of information through advances in communication technology has created a paradox of expectation for marginalised populations around the world. The proliferation of mobile phones on the African continent is ubiquitous in both rural and urban contexts. While Internet penetration is low, those savvy youth who are able to download media from the US, Europe, Nigeria and Ghana sell bootlegged media at their stands, and advertise their wares by broadcasting them in the streets. Walking anywhere around Freetown, you might see a crowd of youth huddled around a generator-powered TV showing Nollywood flicks, or blasting up-to-the-time American Rap videos. In Freetown, one can see hastily scrawled graffiti or homemade T-shirts that place the names of big American acts like Kanye West and Jay-Z alongside popular Sierra Leonean artists such as Kao Denero and LAJ. In the summer of 2011, I saw these names even as far upline as Segbwema in the Kailahun district. This phenomenon not just symbolises increased access to consumer culture, for street youth especially, but also boosts awareness of how others beyond immediate social boundaries are living. As James Ferguson argues, the youth are aware of what membership in modernity entails. When they remain without the basic services that allow modernity to function, such as electricity, running water, access to education, ideas about the gaps in global citizenship are intensified (2006). All over the world, as information is less and less constrained by distance and social realities, the local politically and economically marginalised are integrated into the consumption patterns of the wealthier outside world. This is accompanied by a strengthening of national borders in the North, and an increased division between haves and have-nots within globally connected cities. Claims to belonging through cultural production, through fashion, Facebook pages or musicking practices, and the creation of a collective youth identity are part of a conversation about global integration. Yet even though Sierra Leonean youths are able briefly to transcend their daily realities through participation in a global culture of consumption, the recognition of these youths as equal participants in global society is continually denied.

After the post-election music industry downturn in 2007, many Sierra Leonean artists such as Khady Black and Daddy Saj moved abroad once they were able to do so. These artists then either ended up in obscurity, or attempted to continue nurturing audiences back home and in the diaspora. Several of them have had successful careers in the US and Europe by playing on Sierra Leonean cultural uniqueness. Ahmed Janka Nabay, The Refugee All Stars of Sierra Leone, and Bajah and the Dry Yai Crew (who switched the spelling of their name to Dry Eye Crew for the international market) are marketed to the West by way of the World Music industry. The popularity of Sierra Leonean music in the international industry has been boosted by its position as outsider music. Western marketing teams often play on the Western and African dichotomy, reinforcing a position of cultural other. Even if groups still make songs for the Sierra Leonean market, as Bajah and Dry Yai Crew do, the songs are strategically targeted and markedly different in their aesthetic approach. I recently spent an afternoon with Bajah in my Brooklyn apartment mastering songs that he had produced and recorded on his own and wanted to send home for release on the Sierra Leonean market. These songs were reminiscent of the style I had heard being produced in Sierra Leone in 2006. This occurred at time when Bajah was working on an album in a professional American studio for release on National Geographic's World Music label. The music for the National Geographic project has a much more highly polished international sound. Clearly Bajah and the Dry Yai (Eye) Crew are speaking to two distinct audiences, and as yet they seem to be the only artists attempting to do so.

If there is a desire to be integrated into the global pop conversation, why wouldn't those artists that successfully achieve more global integration, such as the world-festival touring Sierra Leone Refugee Allstars or Ahmed Janka Nabay and The Bubu Gang (a band made up of middle-class white Americans) be more celebrated by Sierra Leonean youth? I suggest it perhaps has to do with Sierra Leonean notions of global citizenship, and the desire of Sierra Leonean youth to be accepted as equals on a transforming global stage. As Stasik argues, a main reason for the post-election decline in the popularity of locally produced music was its association with an electoral politics that failed to deliver on promises of social change, causing local audiences to lose their taste for both. I would like to expand on that reasoning to suggest that local music with a low production quality and a uniquely Sierra Leonean identity was slowly becoming less interesting in a world where citizenship is increasingly defined by an individual's level of participation in a transnational culture of consumption. Given the ease of communication, Sierra Leoneans are increasingly integrated into a global pop-culture audience, and this means their tastes are increasingly influenced by music from abroad. Locally produced music was and continues to be hindered by a lack of production quality, failing to stage effects equal to those in the global sphere. Internationally successful Sierra Leonean artists singing *cultural music* and marketed as the exotic other are not able to combat persistent notions of African marginality. The rise in popularity of music from regional neighbours Ghana and Nigeria, with their growing global visibility, aspirational nature and higher production quality, only reinforce these ideas. When P-Square and Bracket came to town, Sierra Leonean music audiences were suddenly reminded of their marginal global position, even among regional neighbours.

This raises an important point about a new power dynamic emerging in Anglophone West Africa. Recently, Nigeria and Ghana have developed robust media industries whose output enjoys increasing international popularity. These countries' films are feverishly consumed in Northern urban centres, and songs from their burgeoning music industries make it on to international pop charts. Music producers in Ghana and Nigeria play with the same mix of sounds that influenced the postwar Sierra Leonean music industry, but increasingly they manifest their take on the Black Atlantic musical milieu through deep bass, stripped down percussion, warm synthesiser sounds and dramatic orchestral builds. Such digital production tools are elements of a contemporary global language of cultural belonging, which is legible in the work of artists from Toronto to Kingston to Atlanta to Seoul. The media industries in both countries are supported by the material gains of their large diasporas and growing middle classes. The content of the music focuses on themes of love and materialism, reflecting the realities and concerns of these audiences, or the aspirational desires of those who aren't yet among them. The financial resources and networks available to these countries' artists allow them to secure guest appearances from major international artists, such as Snoop Dogg (in Nigerian singer D'Banj's *Mr. Endowed*) or Rick Ross (in Akon signees P-Square's *Beautiful Onyinye*), adding to their international appeal. Members of the diaspora in places like London and New York with influence as tastemakers multiply the awareness and popularity of their country of origin's creative output. In courting the growing buying power of these diasporas, US-based media companies such as Black Entertainment Television (BET) have increasingly included African content in their mainstream programming (Tucker 2011b).

Today, the new Afro-pop sound from West Africa has helped blur the lines between Africa and the West by both borrowing from and influencing the aesthetics of artists in Northern capitals. By tracing the lineage of various genres that have grown in recent years, one can get a sense of the transnational nature of emerging pop cultural dialogues. In recent years, a genre called Funky House has grown in popularity among Black British audiences in London, reputedly because it merged West African and Caribbean rhythms with electronic dance music aesthetics, thus representing the audience's multicultural experiences. A UK-based artist of mixed Ghanaian and Caribbean heritage named Donaeo started experimenting with the sound, and his song "Party Hard" became a major hit in the UK, Ghana and all over Europe and West Africa. Artists in Ghana started experimenting with the same production aesthetics and techniques, and when a new dance craze called Azonto was born, the music associated with it sounded fairly close in production aesthetics to Funky House. The Azonto dance craze then made its way back to London, the new sound riding on the back of the dance, and a specifically Ghanaian take on Funky House became popular all over Africa, Europe and North America. Today, you can find Azonto-inspired songs made by non-African producers in places as unexpected as the Czech Republic, and Azonto dance competitions occur among diaspora populations in places such as the UK, Denmark and Germany (Tucker 2011a). Nigerians also had a crack at the sound, and in 2012 D'Banj's "Oliver Twist" topped British charts. The video for the song, his first after the singer signed up with American producer Kanye West's G.O.O.D. music label, featured a host of American celebrity guest appearances. It is this global context that makes this so-called party music political: it is able to introduce the subjectivities of a group that had seemingly been one-way consumers of culture imported from the West. Commercial pop culture reconfigured notions of North-South cultural flow, and has been able to dismantle the idea of cultural other.

Yet this inclusion in global membership is not automatic for all Africans. Mirroring the growing global influence of neoliberalism, the advances by music industries in wealthier African countries have a splintering effect, and retrench the position of those on the economic margins who cannot compete at the same level. The technical quality of Ghanaian and Nigerian pop cultural products, and the global attention they are able to garner, sets these two West African giants alongside the US, the UK and Jamaica in the Sierra Leonean collective imagination. So Sierra Leonean artists, such as X-Project and Jimmy B, move to Nigeria and Ghana to gain access to the networks and resources that can further their careers. Lesser-name Sierra Leonean artists intentionally incorporate Nigerian phrases into their songs, hoping to make inroads into the bigger market. And Sierra Leonean youths imitate Nigerian fashion and choose Nigerian music over local productions. For Sierra Leonean youth, the pathways to social mobility, both real and imagined, continue to exist outside their local context. In places where there is continued denial of belonging due to the persistent lack of resources and social mobility, the incorporation of the aesthetics of commercial music that speaks of love, partying and materialism into one's outward appearance, daily routine and worldview can be a potent vehicle for introducing new ideas about youth's place in society.

Given these emerging dynamics of the re-imagining of West African global membership, it only makes sense that marginalised Sierra Leonean youth would turn to the most commercially successful form of Black popular music for inspiration, American Gangsta Rap. Gangsta Rap became an international phenomenon in the 1990s when California-based Rappers started flipping the images of dangerous young Black men seen on the nightly news in America, turning them into personal narratives of street survival (NBC Nightly News 1993). This music and cultural aesthetic, a clear political expression of marginalised American youth, would eventually be co-opted by corporate America and become the most lucrative subsection of the growing global Hip Hop market. The images of materialism, individualism, sex, misogyny, drugs and violence would become standard representations of male Blackness in the global imagination, informing Black male identity for generations to come. The rise of Gangsta Rap in the world coincided with the outbreak of the civil war in Sierra Leone. As we have seen, the rebel-thug figure of Tupac was of central importance on the Sierra Leonean battlefield (Jörgel 2008). As we will see, the adaptation of American gang culture remains a very real strategic form of social engagement for marginalised youth in Freetown.

Today, the commercial success of American Gangsta Rap has proven to be socially transformative for many of its former practitioners. Artists such as Jay-Z, Snoop Dogg, Ice Cube and Ice-T, all of whom used to relay messages about the violent aspects of American ghetto life, are now very rich and successful entrepreneurs doing business in several retail and entertainment industries. A former mid-level Brooklyn drug dealer, Jay-Z especially represents a movement from the social margins to the centre of power. Today, he regularly campaigns for Barack Obama and counts the US president among his circle of friends. The content of contemporary commercial American Rap moves away from ghetto tales and leans towards the celebration of a new moneyed middle and upper class lifestyle. All of this boosts the appeal of the American Rap industry for Sierra Leonean youth as the ultimate vehicle for social advancement through participation in global capitalism. It is telling that Kao Denero himself moved to Atlanta, the epicentre of the new Black American middle and upper classes, to further his career. It only makes sense that this American take on Black middle class ascendancy is the vehicle through which the *rarray boys* and the ex-combatants of Freetown can now manifest their dreams, hopes, desires for a different position in the social folds of Sierra Leone.

Unlike the major international Sierra Leonean artists making waves in the World Music industry, the main audience for Sierra Leonean Gangsta Rap music are Sierra Leoneans, even for those artists based abroad. Most artists who are popular locally remain almost totally unknown outside Sierra Leone or the diaspora. This is not abnormal for countries with large diasporas. What is perhaps new or unusual, and reflecting the same trends that have influenced the music scenes in Ghana and Nigeria, is the immediacy of the impact that diaspora-based Rappers are able to enjoy. Through the online distribution of audiovisual content and interactions on social media sites, diaspora Rappers tailor their messages and quickly communicate with audiences back home. As the LAJ car dealership video shows, many of these messages play into fantasies about the lifestyle abroad. The Rappers embody the common dream to go abroad and advance one's life through the opportunities that those far-away places purport to promise (Jackson 2004: 171, Stasik 2011: 129). Adding to these fantasies is the annual ritualised phenomenon of the Sierra Leonean diaspora's holiday visit. These "visiting relatives," identified locally as *JCs* or Just Comes, are Sierra Leoneans who come back home and display various signs of the material success achieved abroad. These temporary residents are met with contradictory feelings by locals, who are suspicious of their outsider status, but look up to their social and economic successes. Stasik notes that by moving to the US, Kao Denero's image

> ... converted from an early local forerunner of a new music trend originating from the US to an embodiment of this very trend and its concomitant imaginary of a new lifestyle ... Since the late 1990's, Kao institutionalized a visiting-relation with his Freetownian followers. In the course of time, his annual visits became a ritualized sermonizing of the newest hip hop trends. (Stasik 2011: 128–9)

Even though Kao has admitted that life in America is not as easy as people in Sierra Leone believe, this is difficult for his fans back home to understand. Most Sierra Leoneans want to believe a better future is possible and available to them if they can just secure a US or UK visa. Additionally, his music and video content continually portray America as a land of wealth. For example, in the video for "Lae We Dance"[5] we see Kao and his Black Leo associates arrive in a Cadillac Escalade at a cabin in the woods in the middle of a snowstorm. They are wearing chinchilla coats and Kao Raps and are surrounded by women, drinks and partying friends. Most often the depictions of struggle in his and other Rappers' songs are reserved for descriptions of life in Sierra Leone and are in stark contrast to the portrayals of the US.

The realities that Rappers deal with in their adopted homes are not totally disconnected from their musical and visual output. While the portrayal of their material realities might not be totally honest, the need to incorporate a hard gangster image could well be informed by the context of these Rappers as immigrants trying to eke out an existence in a sometimes unfriendly society. When they move to the UK, many Sierra Leoneans live in the rougher areas of South and East London. In the US, they may end up in poorer neighbourhoods of cities like New York, Philadelphia, Baltimore and Washington DC. There is a perception, especially in majority African-American neighbourhoods in American inner-cities, that fresh-off-the-boat African immigrants are weak and passive victims of violence (Dolnick 2009). By appropriating a Gangsta Rap aesthetic, Sierra Leonean Rappers are communicating to non-Sierra Leonean Gangsta Rap fans that Africans can be tough. The largest Sierra Leonean diaspora population in the US is in Maryland, in majority African-American areas

---

5. http://youtu.be/CW6J_SPOuDk

such as Prince Georges County and Baltimore. Living in these neighbourhoods, the likes of LAJ or Kao Denero would be very aware of these perceptions of Africa, and the tensions that exist between African-Americans and African immigrants. Perhaps Sierra Leonean Gangsta Rappers incorporate violent aesthetics to counter notions of a cultural other emanating from the African-American communities they live in. Regardless of the audience, by appropriating Gangsta Rap aesthetics Sierra Leonean youth seek to counter prevailing notions about Africa and Africans' place in the world.

While the appropriation of Gangsta aesthetics among Sierra Leonean Rappers and their audience speaks to notions of membership in global society, it is important to remember that these aesthetics inform local social and cultural norms in myriad ways as well. Prevailing opinion on the adaptation of these styles and behaviours from the US is that they have a corrupting influence. However, further investigation reveals that aspects of this marginalised youth culture are easily adapted to Sierra Leonean understandings of oppositional youth identity in a local political context. The first clear precedent is in the *ode-lay* masquerades during the Siaka Stevens regime. The ideas incubated during this time informed youth participation in the violent upheaval during the civil war, and it was during the war that American Gangsta Rap culture of the 1990s, with its individualism, fearlessness and intimidating aspects, was adapted by youth fighters both symbolically and strategically. Before the elections of 2007, a more peaceful but explicitly political oppositional identity emerged, and locally produced music started to play an integral role in party politics. However, when the APC failed to deliver the promised social change (at least immediately), audiences rejected electoral politics and the music that had become so closely associated with it. Today in Sierra Leone, this disillusionment is accompanied by hyper-awareness of the lack of membership in the social realities that constitute contemporary modern existence. In response, Sierra Leonean youth have again turned to American-influenced Gangsta Rap aesthetics, and the nihilism, violence and bravado that accompany it, to represent their worldview. Once they have come on to the scene, Rappers popular locally have to keep a precarious balance between the interests of their fans and of political elites. Beyond just mimicking a Western style that speaks to notions of global membership, the adaptation of these symbolic elements by Rappers and their followers continues to be a strategic form of social and political navigation.

American gang culture imported on the back of Gangsta Rap has become an important tool for social navigation today, partly because of its ease of adaptation to the informal social youth networks that already exist in Sierra Leone. A report on the Freetown riots of December 2010 by journalist Abdul Karim Fonti Kabia identifies the adoption of American-influenced names by "gangster and cultic movements," such as "Members of Blood (MOB), Cent Coast Crips (CCC), and East Rude Clique" (2010). For the socially marginalised around the world, street gangs have provided a form of social navigation in a difficult world of poverty-induced uncertainty. For Sierra Leonean youth surviving on the streets of Freetown away from familial social networks in rural areas, participation in American-informed gang culture is perhaps a low-threshold means of securing the safety and support that the ode-lays, trade unions, wartime networks or political party affiliations are also able to provide. The codes, rituals and symbolic cues such as colours, names and handshakes borrowed from abroad provide convenient entry points to membership in a local support network, and work as a social glue that integrates notions of global belonging. Nunley writes that the *ode-lays* of the 1970s also integrated global language into their local traditions, incorporating everything from kung-fu flicks to Buddha masks into their society's aesthetics, and perhaps, most significant, politically Rastafarian culture and Reggae. They also took names influenced by popular films and current events, such as one *ode-lay* group's adoption of Bloody Mary from the film *OSS Mission 17: Bloody Mary Operation Lotus Flower*. Nunley saw these foreign elements as both symbolically and strategically employed by *ode-lay* participants, and very much in line with local understandings of cultural production (1982). Utas and Jörgel's analysis of the adaptation of American Gangsta Rap aesthetics in war stands out as well. Rebel soldiers during the war would *fearful themselves* by adopting foreign accents, painting Gangsta images on their vehicles and blasting Gangsta Rap when heading into battle. Sometimes, solely based on the association of these things with violence, soldiers would clear out a village without firing a single bullet (2008).

The return and centrality of American gang culture among youth in postwar Sierra Leone is accompanied, and perhaps directly influenced by, the increased popularity of diaspora-produced Rap music. As argued above, Sierra Leonean engagement with Rap music speaks to ideas of global membership and participation. The growing popularity of the genre was aided by the mass disillusionment with locally produced, explicitly political music. It was at this moment that Rappers such as Kao Denero and LAJ could come to prominence among music audiences in Sierra Leone. During the vibrant, postwar industry boom, Rap wasn't as popular as the Afropop and Caribbean-influenced dance sounds produced by artists such as Succulent, Daddy Saj and Emmerson under Jimmy B's tutelage. Instead, it was more of an "underground" scene where young people would host Rap battles among themselves to determine supremacy. Even if Sierra Leonean artists such as The Jungle Leaders, Pupa Bajah and Baw Waw Society Rapped in their songs, their most popular numbers tended to incorporate rhythms and themes associated with a more pan-African identity (Bah 2010). The orientation of postwar popular music illustrated a burgeoning cultural and national pride in the immediate aftermath of the 1992 coup that ousted Joseph Momoh. After the election of 2007, Kao especially saw his popularity grow as he was able to embody the escapism Sierra Leonean audiences were by then seeking. He skilfully flowed in Krio over more Americanised beats, incorporated American-influenced themes of individualism, consumerism and bravado, and adopted American attitude, style and swagger. As Sierra Leonean music audiences began to look increasingly to cultural production from outside their local context as the place to locate their dreams of social advancement, Philadelphia-based Kao Denero would ironically come to embody the title "King of Freetown."

While not treating explicitly political themes, Rappers such as Kao Denero create music and affect a style that speak to the political claims of marginalised Sierra Leonean youth. First, because of their bravado and affectation of material wealth, these Rappers can assume the status of having become *big men* among their peers. A *big man* is a central figure in a formal or informal network who controls and distributes resources and takes tribute as political patronage (Utas 2012). Rappers exemplify this role among their immediate crews as explained by Bah in the *Sierra Express Media* newspaper:

> Most of the artists today are employing at least 20 to 30 youths to run their affairs ... Most of [these youths], if not for this venture, would be in the streets somewhere smoking weed all day or doing other drugs. The same goes for LAJ, Pupa Baja and many other artists. They all have serious influence in young people across all regional or tribal boundaries, and if they are assisted properly, can make an enormous difference. (2010)

Beyond this very practical reasoning, the ability of Rappers to embody this role is important symbolically for the political claims of marginalised youth. Just as in the 1970s with Super Combo and Afro National, individual Rappers have become nodes in extended networks of youth to mobilise around. This symbolism is especially relevant to the various Gangsta crews that have sprung up around Freetown, which share aesthetic influences with the Rappers and their immediate crew members. The various crews mentioned in reports of the December riots were supposedly affiliated with a corresponding Rapper and his crew, in this case LAJ's Red Flag Movement and Menace Da General's West Africa Movement (Kabia 2010). Fans of the Rappers are so enthusiastic in their support that they are able to shut down parts of the city when one of the artists arrives on the ferry from Lungi airport.[6] When these crowds engage in violent behaviour, they can send waves of fear through the greater population. The political significance of these gatherings lies in their ability to demonstrate to the public the latent mass mobilising power inherent in Sierra Leonean youth culture.

The appearance of Rappers as *big men* able to mobilise masses of youth is a clear realisation of Rancière's theory of political dissensus. The mobilisation of marginalised youth around non-traditional figures introduces new ideas about norms of social control and who in society is fit for ruling (Corcoran 2010: 30–1). Also, in a society that often denies the right to political speech by marginalised youth, such mass gatherings are a way for them to assert their existence. As a mobilising force, such gatherings also have potential – as yet

---

6. http://youtu.be/EX371Ve_Erg

unrealised – as a vehicle for youth to make explicit political claims, just as the *ode-lays* did for youth rebellion throughout the 1970s and 1980s. Even without an explicit political agenda, the Rappers today challenge the status quo by being able enact the appearance of political power and wealth without going through the normal channels associated with an elder-youth hierarchy. The American Rap-influenced lifestyle is based on individualism and social mobility through sometimes nefarious means. For Sierra Leonean street youth, engagement with this culture is an important political statement, because it suggests a new and preferred vision for Sierra Leone's future. This is a future in which a youth, or marginalised member of society, can become socially mobile, even a *big man* in Sierra Leone without entering into formal political alliances or going through other traditional channels. This is in direct contradiction to the accepted norms of social mobility that political elites and traditional elders aim to reinforce, especially in the wake of a violent rebellion in which the youth were major participants.

Exploring the parallels between Rappers as central figures in an informal network of marginalised youth and the *devil* figures of the *ode-lay* societies can give us further insight into the local meaning of Gangsta Rap culture in Sierra Leone. The fierceness and bravado common to Rap music and American gang culture are of central importance to *ode-lay* performances. Also, music has always played a central role in these masquerades, and high skills among accompanying musicians was integral to the masquerade's success . Whenever they visit from the spiritual realm, the *devils'* visit is temporary, just as the Rappers' visit from abroad is temporary. The followers of the *devils* act out some of the wider social forces at play and aim to use the *devil* for various means, whether to promote peace or defeat an enemy (Utas 2008). The same perhaps can be said of the followers of various Rap crews in events like the December riots.

The position of Rappers in society as *big men* also speaks to contemporary ideas of witchcraft in Sierra Leone, adding an element of nefariousness to their reputation. According to Rosalind Shaw, the *witch* figure is one that is able to access an "urban world of wealth and rapid global mobility" through mysterious and mainly immoral means (1997: 857). These ideas were formed over time through Sierra Leone's integration into the transatlantic slave trade, and the belief that European wealth, or the wealth of those tapped into global capitalism, was derived from the sacrifice of (mostly poor and socially marginalised) Africans to malevolent spiritual beings. These beliefs have been transformed in contemporary society to characterise those able to access wealth through dubious means, and many of the aesthetics of witchcraft mythology continue to incorporate ideas of Western wealth and connection to global networks of trade. Such ideas contribute to a belief in the general immorality of North American culture (Shaw 1997, 2001). This belief perhaps contributes to the vilification of

American Gangsta Rap culture in the greater society, and is a possible explanation of why rebel soldiers were able to integrate American cultural aesthetics into their *fearful yourself* technique during the war. Finally, perhaps the most important parallel between Rappers, *devils* and *witches* is their shared place in urban society as sites of alternative political contestation and social mobility.

Understanding Rappers as either *devil* figures or symbolic *big men* can also give insight into the motivation, as well as the social ramifications, of the beef that has arisen between Rappers throughout the years. As identified by Taylor, one mode of securing one's hold over power in Sierra Leonean politics is through the elimination and displacement of rival *big men* and their patronage networks. Since the lead-up to the election of 2007, rivalry between parties has reached fever pitch, and securing political office has become a high-stakes game of total win or loss (Taylor 2009). These strategies to secure political power are, again, easily adapted to the idea of Rap beef originating in American Hip Hop culture. To remain relevant, Rappers must engage in the same strategies of elimination and support employed by political *big men*, albeit metaphorically. Rappers are most able to secure their reputations and eliminate opponents through lyrical skill destroying the opponents' reputation, but also by adopting the aesthetics of wealth and acting out a public persona that reinforces their toughness. This need to reinforce one's reputation mirrors observations made by John Nunley about the *ode-lay* devils of the 1980s. Nunley argued that press coverage of masquerade events often shapes public perceptions of individual societies. Displays of fierceness would earn individual societies reputations for unruliness and violence, but also bravery. Police would often clamp down on the most notorious societies' activities, and groups gained kudos for standing strong against attempts at enforcement and regulation. Additionally, local media were able to shape reputations of fierceness, and societies tried to live up to press reports in ensuing masquerades. Tracking a specific society's reputation even became an important post-masquerade ritual (Nunley 1988). Today, the followers of Rappers are just as engaged in securing their crew's reputation as the *ode-lays* are and were, and there is no doubt that the local press retains a central role in shaping such reputations.

In the months after the beef between Kao Denero and LAJ was initiated, the Red Flag Movement seemed to nurture its reputation for being unpredictable and prone to violence. Particularly notable was the tragic decision of a Red Flag Movement associate to carry a gun to a beachfront nightclub in Freetown in January 2012. After getting into a fight with an up-and-coming Rapper named Big Fish inside the club, the associate was reported to have fired gunshots into the air. An ensuing car chase and subsequent crash on Lumley Beach resulted in the deaths of three people. Both LAJ and Big Fish were charged with felonies, and spent time in prison (Coker 2012, Sham 2012). The Red Flag Movement's association with violent behaviour is perhaps directly influenced by the aesthetics the crew chose to adopt. The Red Flag Movement wears red, and many of LAJ's videos involve visual imagery similar to that in videos of the American gang The Bloods. As noted during the war, and evident in the adaptation of gang names, codes and cues by urban youth today, Sierra Leoneans are very aware of the reputation of the American Bloods. While this association can bolster a reputation and increase popularity, just as the political messages in music observed by Shepler in 2007 did, an inauthentic association can damage one's reputation. The top Youtube comment on LAJ's "Propeller" video (as of 13 March 2012) uses this idea of authenticity against LAJ, "yo this niga a fake ass niga ... aint no bloods in sierra leone... we dont do that shit cuz, that not our style ... and your bitch ass better never come down to philly cuz ... cuz you gonna get serve pussy."[7] Kao Denero also uses this point as fodder for a diss aimed at LAJ by saying, "you just yappin'/actin' like you built for this/pretendin' you a Blood/you might get killed for this." Regardless of the authenticity of their portrayal of a gangster image, the association of the Red Flag Movement with the Bloods certainly ups the ante in their behavioural choices.

While direct violent opposition to the state and its hierarchical apparatus has yet to form in Sierra Leone's postwar period, the continued appearance of public violence still creates unease among many Sierra Leoneans about the prospects for peace. As with the meaning behind the assembling of youths into massive crowds, the adaptation of violent aesthetics by marginalised youth can be a form of political speech. In Sierra Leone today, the most notorious violence is that associated with party political campaigning. Youth often play a central role in this violence as foot soldiers for political *big men*. In the public's mind, tension between Rap crews that comes out in this environment creates an atmosphere conducive to violent behaviour, and can be seen as both reminder of past violence and a precursor of future instability. The state thus has no choice but to pay attention to the Gangsta Rap phenomenon, since the appearance of violence directly threatens the social order necessary to secure state-building resources. When Rappers enact a *big man* image, they also invoke a figure able to control and manipulate youth violence. So the Rappers' influence on the masses of marginalised youth in the country makes them important stakeholders in the future development of the country. This also makes them an easy scapegoat when public violence breaks out. For the marginalised youth, their impact on the public psyche through acts of violence is not lost on them. Indeed, it often remains the ultimate resource in their claims to equality and rights as political speakers.

Along with the continued oppositional youth identity channelled through Gangsta Rap aesthetics is the continued potential to police youth by incorporating them into political parties and the state apparatus. Before there was

---

7.   http://www.youtube.com/user/vugaman01

ever any Rap beef in Freetown, political party machines used youth violence to further their political aims (Abdullah 1997, 2005, Rosen 2005, Christensen and Utas 2008). Today, the state continues its attempts at control through either eliminating or co-opting the competition, and privileging supporters. These strategies can be easily deployed through popular music audiences, as seen in the party-fabricated rivalry between Emmerson and Innocent. While there is no direct evidence, such dynamics may well be playing out among today's crop of Gangsta Rap-influenced artists. When it comes to Rappers, the government has been able to eliminate threats in various ways. One, tapping into traditional modes of social management, is the mediation of the beef by an elder, partly to restore social order, but also for that elder to retain some sort of political authority. When tensions arise in Sierra Leone, the government steps in to create agreement between parties. This reinforces its position as having control over society, and particularly a monopoly on violence. This symbolic roll of the elder is not limited to Sierra Leone proper. When tensions developed in the diaspora, Sierra Leone community members in Washington DC employed similar strategies of mediation. However, when actual violence breaks out, this strategy may not be the most effective for restoring social order. In this case, a second strategy is employed, total elimination of the threat. The attempt by government officials to control public violence could be seen in December 2010 when the government banned all music performances. This they did to ease the public mind in the wake of youth rioting, and to give the appearance of control over violence in the public sphere.

A more subtle way in which politicians and press can downplay a threat to social order is by categorising public speech acts by youth as devoid of political meaning. This strategy entails refusing to recognise the public speech acts of marginalised populations as valid, of equal stature, or as proper to the realm of politics. President Koroma exemplified this in a speech at a free concert in the national stadium in Freetown to celebrate approval of the Sierra Leonean anti-piracy law. LAJ, out on bail for the nightclub incident on Lumley Beach, was scheduled to perform, so many of his supporters were in the audience. Before LAJ took the stage, his supporters threw bottles of urine and other liquids at police. The latter responded with pepper spray. This confrontation would seem to be a clear example of the fierceness and bravado that also characterised the *ode-lay*, displays that have historically carried political meaning. After LAJ finished performing, President Koroma took the stage and said:

"Let's all agree to say no to violence in the music industry as well as during our upcoming elections, everyone has a role to play in the transformation of Sierra Leone". He also added that everyone should feel free to vote for their representative of choice and that everyone should have a voice and a vote ... The President congratulated the organizers and musicians for a job well done and he said that he understood that the incident that happened earlier with the Police was as a result of "over excitement". He left with fanfare and applause. (Sesay 2012)

By categorising the LAJ supporters' clash with police as "over excitement," the president showed he wouldn't recognise such acts as speech on par with the political displays incorporating fierceness enacted by his own party and its rivals. This is reminiscent of the strategies employed by the state-controlled media, which both demonised and vaunted different societies during the Siaka Stevens regime, according to whether they were in favour or not (Nunley 1982). Is this public equivalent of saying "They're just kids having fun" and meant to neutralise the political potential of the Red Flag Movement? Perhaps it is meant as a show of indirect support, a gesture of amnesty for the movement's members.

Given the history of the co-option of youth into political parties, it is no surprise that some members of the public perceive a direct connection between the Red Flag Movement and the APC, both of whose colours are red. While this association has not been corroborated, the visual similarities at public gatherings between the two are noteworthy. The association is close enough for LAJ to assume his detention after the beach shooting was a politically motivated move by the SLPP (Cham 2012). In a 2011 interview with Salone Jamboree, LAJ denies a direct relationship between himself and the APC, but his answer does not completely dispel such association. He said: "He is not a politician and does not have close friends in the APC party either; but he affirmed: 'If the APC party continues like this, I will end up voting for them in 2012 elections'" (Salone Jamboree, 2010e). In the context of Sierra Leonean political history, it wouldn't be too farfetched to believe there might be an unseen hand at work through the APC to finance or promote the Red Flag Movement. The conflation of violence, citizenship and democracy in Sierra Leone means an association with the Red Flag Movement and its reputation for violence could be a useful campaigning tool. Utas and Christensen explain the relationship between violence and politics in their analysis of the 2007 elections:

> Violent encounters not only fueled conflict between opposing factions but also came to be closely intertwined with notions of rights and citizenship ... rationales were articulated by task force members arguing that as citizens of Sierra Leone it was their right to influence the election results – not only by casting their own votes but also by sensitizing other people to vote for a certain candidate. Here, the campaigning went far beyond "ordinary sensitization" and participation in rallies to using violence to force people to vote for certain candidates. (2008: 533–4)

With legions of youth roaming the streets in the ruling party's colours, and with suppressed memories of similar youth terrorising the town during the civil war, it's difficult to imagine the APC would not benefit from their existence. Because of the behaviour of the Red Flag Movement and their close association with the APC, some citizens may even feel forced to vote for the APC solely to maintain peace. Regardless, the government's perceived control over the APC would signal that they are a strong force, able to maintain influence over perhaps Freetown's fiercest youth group.

Adding fuel to such rumours are the common modes of social navigation whereby one disguises one's intentions by appearing to act out one's prescribed social role (Jackson 2004: 136, Abdullah 2007, Christensen and Utas 2008). Individuals are expected to embody their role through interaction with other people. As mentioned above, traditional beliefs allow for the contestation of social roles through cultural performances such as initiation ceremonies. These forms of contestation are intimately tied to spiritual beliefs, which suggest that the masks worn by various secret societies contain hidden information that only the wearer can absorb. Such esoteric information is seen as highly valuable and becomes an essential mode of social navigation (Ferme 2001). While dressing up in the latest global trends says something about belonging to a global consumer society, it also speaks to some Sierra Leoneans' beliefs about the ability of dress and masks to temporarily embody and transcend social roles. Beliefs about social transformation are born out of the long history of the transatlantic slave trade, and connected to ideas of human leopards, human crocodiles and human chimpanzees. Rather than being primitive or backward manifestations of culture, these modes of understanding are in direct response to the forces integrating Sierra Leone into a system of global capitalism (Shaw 2001). Thus, modes of social navigation that involve hiding one's intentions have become common in business dealings, as well as in the national politics of Sierra Leone.

The uncertainties on the political surface allow for the manipulation of political symbols such as Rappers, sometimes beyond their own intended meaning. What is important here is the symbolic political meaning of Rappers for marginalised youth. The Rappers become important public figures and serve as vehicles through which youth are able to channel their subjectivities. Thus, such figures can enact a politics of dissensus whether they intend to or not (Hoffman 2006). At the same time, this is why Rappers and others can be, and have been, co-opted by the policing regime. Rappers are caught between the desire of youth to become political speakers and politicians wanting to police the social order. When Rappers have been co-opted by a political party, yet have hidden this to safeguard their reputations, a dynamic is created that causes them to send contradictory messages regarding their relationship with violence. Kao Denero starts out many of his beef songs with a disclaimer that he doesn't mean to perpetuate violence, and then goes on to depict violent imagery in the elimination of his opponents. Whenever a music event triggers violence, the Rappers involved always seem remorseful and try to dissociate themselves from the trouble. A Kao Denero quote illustrates his precarious position:

> I wish [LAJ] well, I felt betrayed and used. That's all. I'm a clean-hearted individual but sometimes I don't get back the same in return. The position I find myself in makes me a target for unwanted drama so now I just shake it off and ignore. No more free promotion for cats. LOL. (Politicosl 2012)

Although he constantly states he doesn't want any part in violence and sees it as hurting Sierra Leone, he still needs to maintain a *big man* image to secure his reputation. Politicians are well-known for employing similar contradictory tactics in their political navigations. A political party may have a head who speaks about peace to the press, while party members employ task forces to carry out violent political campaigning.

The final way in which politicians can police potential political voice by youth is through their incorporation into peace campaigns, a strategy successfully employed by NGOs in the postwar period. On Easter weekend 2012, President Koroma presided over a truce between Kao Denero and LAJ.[8] The truce was formally announced at the annual *East vs. West* music competition at the national stadium in Freetown (Remoe 2012). To gain control over violence in the country in the run-up to the elections of 2012 the government of Sierra Leone launched a "Say No to Violence" campaign. The recruitment of the country's two biggest Rap stars for the campaign speaks volumes about the power Rappers have been able to appropriate through their ability to rally youth. The two Rappers names also appeared in the title of a Youtube video called "Save Mama Salone" by the T-Town Allstars,[9] which also featured a host of other artists. In the introduction to the video, the director of the Save Mama Salone Foundation can be seen travelling the country asking for messages of peace from key public figures. Just like Tupac and the Notorious B.I.G., LAJ and Kao Denero are two symbols of violence that were easily co-opted and turned into symbols of peace. An opinion piece by Ismael Bayoh on the news blog *Politicosl.com* asks, who is really benefiting from these messages of peace? His observations provide insight into the suspicions that continue to surround political manoeuvring in Sierra Leone, and are worth quoting at length:

> I am compelled to write this piece after close observations of how some people are using the name and influence of our musicians in their so called campaign against violence as we approach the November 17th, 2012 multi-tier elections … Musicians can definitely play a pivotal role in campaigns and by the way, Artistes for Peace are doing such campaigns. This campaign is totally differ-

---

8. http://youtu.be/kLKUMRLy1r8
9. http://youtu.be/mIGaXmokMig

ent from this new campaign now bandied around from the National Stadium to Attouga and back to the stadium with the theme "say no to violence". The first stadium show hosted, the President was invited as guest of honor in that campaign, and the artistes were rallied because of their fan base for motives best known to the organizers. Most of the organizers were in red lacoste projecting their image in flamboyance against the talents of the artistes. I pondered around when the musicians have become the beacon of violence in Sierra Leone politics ... One question keeps playing around that why is it that in the campaigns for non violence as we approach the elections, the President is the sole politician invited as guest of honour ... [W]e all know that violence persists during OG contests, football gala matches, sports meet. Presently, rap is giving a different intention to the public by some people ... What is amusing is how these artistes have accepted the nomenclature of violence among their fans when they fully well know that political violence is perpetrated by either the SLPP or APC. Has the tussle between Black Leo and RFM [Red Flag Movement] warranted the Political Affairs Minister and the President to host them at State House if not for other motives? (2012)

Conclusion

Rancière's definition of politics is a useful frame through which to view Sierra Leone, because it recognises the political agency of all parts of the population. Recognising the political voice of youth through Gangsta Rap in Sierra Leone is one way of expanding the definition of democracy in the country. Those interested in pursuing modes of democratic inclusion around the world, not just in Sierra Leone, need to understand that forms of participation integrated into a consensus regime are inherently exclusive. Unlike concerns such as health, security and formal education, youth cultural production is only given serious attention when it seems to interfere with those other concerns. The modes of participation that marginalised populations choose to engage in can tell us more about their visions of what the future should look like than those modes prescribed by experts. If policy-makers ignore marginalised populations' agency, they will never be able to connect with them in real and meaningful ways.

Globally, forms of youth cultural production such as Hip Hop have been manipulated by both state and market to serve their own ends (Aidi 2011). In Sierra Leone's postwar years, politicians undermined an important political dynamic of postwar youth culture by co-opting the local music industry. However, this decline in local industry did not dismantle youth political subjectivity as a subaltern identity. The failures of the reintegration programme in Sierra Leone lie in the inability to provide alternatives for social mobility and the ability to contest citizenship outside state politics. In places where the infrastructure is not equipped to deal with the expectations of youth, alternative means of youth engagement need to be employed. If there are no jobs in traditional industries, then the state and civil society need to be proactive in creating alternative means of employment. If the education system is failing, they need to find alternative means of empowerment through learning. The only way to prevent a recurrence of violence in the society is to allow for and nurture alternative modes of political disagreement.

An alternative development trajectory might look at the community infrastructures that local people have managed to develop without support, and retrofit those infrastructures (Simone 2006, Lindell and Utas 2012). In Sierra Leone, the youth have taken up the occupations of musician, athlete, motorbike taxi driver, *poda poda* bus crew member, informal market trader, and mercenary for hire in local politics and foreign wars. Some of these occupations are tools for building a more peaceful and stable society, while others are more destructive. Forms of constructive societal contribution, such as the forms of speech facilitated by the rise of digital production, need to be recognised as the important claims to citizenship that they are. This should be followed by comprehensive support from both the state and the international community.

The good news is that elsewhere in the world and around Africa democratic movements have emerged through which the marginalised and uncounted have been able to shape global perceptions through claims of equality as political speakers. Senegal is an example where youth were able to organise around culture and encourage the ousting of the incumbent president, Abdoulaye Wade. In Nigeria, youth rallied against corrupt politicians and organised to reinstate state oil subsidies. And in North Africa and around the Arabic-speaking world, youth populations participated in and sometimes initiated uprisings that led to revolution in many countries. Even seemingly apolitical expressions such as Kuduro, Coupe Decale, Baile Funk, Dancehall and Sierra Leonean Rap are important claims to political recognition, and have sometimes brought global attention to the local populations that spawned them. While often those populations have yet to see benefit from such interest, the potential for these expressions to spawn social change remains high. For this to happen in a place like Sierra Leone, solidarity and support will in part have to come from like-minded young people outside the country. My own continued interaction with Sierra Leone will be informed by these realities.

Bibliography

Abdullah, Ibrahim (1997). "Introduction - special issue on Lumpen culture and political violence: the Sierra Leone Civil War." *Africa Development* xxii (3/4):5–18.

Abdullah, Ibrahim (1998). "Bush Path to Destruction: The Origin and Character of the Revolutionary United Front-Sierra Leone." *Journal of Modern African Studies* 36 (2):203–35.

Abdullah, Ibrahim (2005). "'I am a rebel': youth, culture and violence in Sierra Leone," in A. Honwana and F.D. Boeck (eds), *Makers and Breakers: Children and Youth in Postcolonial Africa*. Oxford: James Currey, 172–87.

Abdullah, Ibrahim (2007). "'Nar De Numbah Kill De Bombah': Popular Culture, Subaltern Agency, and Peoples Power." *Cocorioko.net*. Web.

Adolfo, Eldridge and Måns Hanssen (2010). *Sierra Leone: Splitting Under the Strain of Elections?* Stockholm: FOI, Division of Defence Analysis.

Aidi, Hishaam (2011). "The Grand (Hip-Hop) Chessboard Race, Rap and Raison d'État." *Middle East Report* 260:25–39.

Bah, Algassimu Monoma (2010). "Violence in the Sierra Leone Music Industry ... How it Started." *Sierra Express Media*, 19 December. Web. http://www.sierraexpressmedia.com/archives/17719

Bayoh, Ismael (2012). "Who says hip hop music is responsible for violence." *Politicosl.com*, April. Web. http://politicosl.com/2012/04/who-says-hip-hop-music-is-responsible-for-the-violence/

Beah, Ishmael (2007). *A Long Way Gone: Memoirs of a Boy Soldier.* New York: Farrar, Straus and Giroux.

Cham, Kemo (2012). "Sierra Leone rapper in double trouble." *Africa Review,* 27 January. Web. http://www.africareview.com/Arts+and+Culture/Sierra+Leone+rapper+in+double+trouble/-/979194/1314882/-/ysim4az/-/index.html

Christensen, Maya and Mats Utas (2008). "Mercenaries of Democracy: The 'Politricks' of Remobilized Combatants in the 2007 General Elections, Sierra Leone." *African Affairs* 107 (429):515–39.

Christiansen, C., et al. (2006). "Youth(e)scapes: Introduction," in C. Christiansen, M. Utas and H. Vigh (eds), *Navigating youth, generating adulthood: Social becoming in an African context*. Uppsala: Nordic Africa Institute, 9–28.

Corcoran, Steve and Jaques Rancière (2010). *Dissensus: On Politics and Aesthetics.* London and New York: Continuum.

Coker, Femi (2012). "50 million bail for L.A.J. and Big Fish." *Sierra Leone News Hunters,* 24 January. Web. http://www.sierraleonenewshunters.com/content/50-million-bail-laj-big-fish

Cushing, Peter and Chris Parachini (2003). "Gen. Butt Naked vs. The Tupac Army: West Africa Has Gone Mad and It Looks Fantastic!" *Vice Magazine*. Web. http://www.vice.com/read/gen-v10n7

Dolnick, Sam (2009). "For African Immigrants, Bronx Culture Clash Turns Violent." *New York Times*, 19 October. NY/Region Section.

Ellis, Stephen (2007). *The Mask of Anarchy*. London: Hurst and New York: New York University Press.

Fanthorpe, Richard (2001). "Neither citizen nor subject? 'Lumpen' agency and the legacy of native administration in Sierra Leone." *African Affairs* (100):363–86.

Ferguson, James (1999). *Expectations of modernity: Myths and meanings of urban life on the Zambian Copperbelt*. Berkeley CA: University of California Press.

Ferguson, James (2006). *Global shadows: Africa in the neoliberal world order*. Durham NC: Duke University Press.

Ferme, Mariane C. (2001). *The underneath of things: Violence, history, and the everyday in Sierra Leone*. Berkeley CA: University of California Press.

Graham, Stephen, and Simon Marvin (2001). *Splintering Urbanism: Networked Infrastructures, Technological Mobilities and the Urban Condition*. London: Routledge.

Hansen, Kieran (2011). *Shooting Freetown*. Manchester: Granada Centre, University of Manchester. Web Video. http://vimeo.com/33610757

Hoffman, Danny (2006). "Disagreement: Dissent Politics and the War in Sierra Leone." *Africa Today* 52 (3), Spring:3–22.

Jackson, Michael (2004). *In Sierra Leone*. Durham NC: Duke University Press.

Kabia, Abdul Karim Fonti (2010). "In Sierra Leone, Youth Riots in Freetown." *Awareness Times*, 13 December. Web. http://news.sl/drwebsite/exec/view. cgi?archive=6&num=16942

Kaplan, Robert (1994). "The Coming Anarchy." *Atlantic Magazine*, February Edition.

Kraft, Scott (2010). "In Sierra Leone, pop music is a beat that drives politics." *Los Angeles Times*, 3 January. Web. http://articles.latimes.com/2010/jan/03/world/la-fg-africa-music3-2010jan03

Lindell, Ilda and Mats Utas (2012). "Networked city life in Africa: Introduction." *Urban Forum* 23(4):409–14.

Lock, Katrin (2005). "Who is Listening? Sierra Leone, Liberia, and Senegal," in M. Franklin, (ed.), *Resounding International Relations: On Music, Culture, and Society*. New York: Palgrave, 141–60.

Mamdani, Mahmood (1996). *Citizen and Subject: Contemporary Africa and the legacy of late colonialism*. Princeton NJ: Princeton University Press.

Mann, Larisa (2011). "Decolonizing Copyright: Jamaican Street Dances and Globally Networked Technology." *Berkman Center for Internet and Society Podcast*. Boston: Harvard University. Web Video. http://blogs.law.harvard.edu/mediaberkman/2011/03/22/larisa-mann-on-decolonizing-copyright-jamaican-street-dances-and-globally-networked-technology/

Moran, Mary (2006). *Liberia: The Violence of Democracy*. Philadelphia: University of Pennsylvania Press.

NBC Nightly News. (1993). "1993 NBC Report on Gangsta Rap" *Youtube*: GoldenEraTV. Web Video. http://youtu.be/SezuXZGBDJ8

Nunley, John (1981). "The fancy and the fierce." *African Arts* 14(2):52–9.

Nunley, John (1982). "Images and printed words in Freetown masquerades." *African Arts* 15(4):42–6.

Nunley, John (1985). "The lantern festival in Sierra Leone." *African Arts* 18(2):45–9, 97, 102–3.

Nunley, John (1988). "Purity and pollution in Freetown masked performance." *Drama Review* 32(2):102–32.

Opala, J. (1994). "'Ecstatic renovation!': Street art celebrating Sierra Leone's 1992 revolution." *African Affairs* 93(371):195–218.

Panton, Rodney (2006). "The Beautiful Struggle." *BBC Radio One*. London. Web. http://www.bbc.co.uk/radio1/documentaries/20060718_rodneyp.shtml.

Peters, Krjin (2007). "From weapons to wheels: Young Sierra Leonean ex-combatants become motorbike taxi-riders." *Journal of Peace Conflict and Development* 10, March:1–23.

Politicosl (2012). "I Am Relentless – Kao Denero" *Politicosl.com,* February. Web. http://politicosl.com/2012/02/exclusive-interview-with-kao-denero/

Prestholdt, Jeremy (2009). "The afterlives of 2Pac: Imagery and alienation in Sierra Leone." *Journal of African Cultural Studies* 21(2):197–218.

Remoe, Vickie (2012). "LAJ, Denero end hip hop rivalry at concert in Sierra Leone." *Swit Salone,* 13 April. Web. http://www.switsalone.com/15358_l-a-j-denero-end-hip-hop-rivalry-at-concert-in-sierra-leone/

Richards, Paul (1996). *Fighting for the Rainforest: War, Youth and Resources in Sierra Leone.* Portsmouth NH: Heinemann.

Richards, Paul (1999). "Out of wilderness? Escaping Robert Kaplan's dystopia." *Anthropology Today* 15(6):16–18.

Rosen, David M. (2005). *Armies of the young: Child soldiers in war and terrorism.* New Brunswick NJ: Rutgers University Press.

Salone Jamboree (2010a). "And the winner is – Kao Denero." *Sierra Express Media,* 6 July. Web. http://www.sierraexpressmedia.com/archives/10933

Salone Jamboree (2010b). "Government brokers peace between Kao and LAJ" *Salone Jamboree.* Web. http://www.salonejamboree.net/index.php?option=com_content&view=article&id=79:government-brokers-peace-between-kao-and-laj&catid=13:interviews&Itemid=27#.T57NomjVkeA.link

Salone Jamboree (2010c). "I was born to do this – Kao Denero." *Sierra Express Media,* 2 February. Web. http://www.sierraexpressmedia.com/archives/5613

Salone Jamboree (2010d). "LAJ bitter after failing to land hip-hop title." *Sierra Express Media,* 8 July. Web. http://www.sierraexpressmedia.com/archives/11011

Salone Jamboree (2010e). "'Red Flag is not APC ... But I'll Vote APC' – LAJ." *Salone Jamboree.* Web. http://www.salonejamboree.net/index.php?option=com_

content&view=article&id=176:red-flag-is-not-apcbut-ill-vote-apc-laj&catid=1:latest&Itemid=26

Samba, Augustine (2010). "In Sierra Leone, Government Bans Musical Activities ... 78 Rioters Dragged to Court." *Awareness Times*, 14 December. Web. http://news.sl/drwebsite/exec/view.cgi?archive=6&num=16958

Saucier, P. Khalil (2011). *Native Tongues: An African Hip Hop Reader*. Trenton NJ: African World Press.

Sesay, Victoria (2012). "Musicians celebrate new copyrite law in Freetown." *Swit Salone*, 28 February. Web. http://www.switsalone.com/14910_musicians-celebrate-new-copyrite-law-with-free-concert-in-freetown/

Shaw, Rosalind (1997). "The production of witchcraft/witchcraft as production: Memory, modernity, and slave trade in Sierra Leone." *American Ethnologist* 24(4):856–76.

Shaw, Rosalind (2001). "Cannibal transformations: Colonialism and commodification in the Sierra Leone hinterland," in H. Moore and T. Sanders (eds), *Magical interpretations, material realities: modernity, witchcraft and the occult in post-colonial Africa*. London: Routledge, 50–70.

Shepler, Susan (2010). "Youth Music and Politics in Post-war Sierra Leone." *Journal of Modern African Studies* 48(4):627–42.

Simone, AbdouMaliq (2004). "People as Infrastructure: Intersecting Fragments in Johannesburg." *Public Culture* 16(3), Fall:407–29

Stasik, Michael (2011). *DISCOnnections. Popular Music Audiences in Freetown, Sierra Leone*. Leiden: Leiden University Press.

Taylor, Ian (2009). "Earth Calling the Liberals: Locating the Political Culture of Sierra Leone as Terrain for 'Reform.'" *New Perspectives on Liberal Peacebuilding*. Tokyo, New York, Paris: United Nations University Press, 159–77.

Tucker, Boima (2011a). "Azonto Germany." *Africa is a Country*, 23 February. Web. http://africasacountry.com/2012/02/23/azonto-germany/

Tucker, Boima (2011b). "Africa is a Category." *Africa is a Country*, 30 May. Web. http://africasacountry.com/2012/05/30/africa-is-a-category/

Utas, Mats (2007). "Watermelon Politics in Sierra Leone: Hope amidst Vote Buying and Remobilised Militias." *African Renaissance* 4(3/4):62–6.

Utas, Mats (2008). "Abject heroes: Marginalised youth, modernity and violent pathways of the Liberian Civil War," in J. Hart (ed.), *Years of Conflict: Adolescence, Political Violence and Displacement*.Oxford: Berghahn Books, 111–38.

Utas, Mats (2008). *Civili Rule*. Uppsala: Nordic Africa Institute, 2008. Web Video. http://www.nai.uu.se/events/multimedia/civili/#comp0000491500b50000001e7c61ca

Utas, Mats and Jörgel, Magnus (2008). "The West Side Boys: Military navigation in the Sierra Leone civil war." *Journal of Modern African Studies* 46(3):487–511.

Utas, Mats (2012). "Introduction: Bigmanity and network governance in African conflicts," in M. Utas (ed.), *African conflicts and informal power: Big men and networks*. London: Zed Books, 1–34.

CURRENT AFRICAN ISSUES PUBLISHED BY THE INSTITUTE

Recent issues in the series are available electronically
for download free of charge www.nai.uu.se

1981

1. *South Africa, the West and the Frontline States. Report from a Seminar.*

2. Maja Naur, *Social and Organisational Change in Libya.*

3. *Peasants and Agricultural Production in Africa. A Nordic Research Seminar. Follow-up Reports and Discussions.*

1985

4. Ray Bush & S. Kibble, *Destabilisation in Southern Africa, an Overview.*

5. Bertil Egerö, *Mozambique and the Southern African Struggle for Liberation.*

1986

6. Carol B.Thompson, *Regional Economic Polic under Crisis Condition. Southern African Development.*

1989

7. Inge Tvedten, *The War in Angola, Internal Conditions for Peace and Recovery.*

8. Patrick Wilmot, *Nigeria's Southern Africa Policy 1960–1988.*

1990

9. Jonathan Baker, *Perestroika for Ethiopia: In Search of the End of the Rainbow?*

10. Horace Campbell, *The Siege of Cuito Cuanavale.*

1991

11. Maria Bongartz, *The Civil War in Somalia. Its genesis and dynamics.*

12. Shadrack B.O. Gutto, *Human and People's Rights in Africa. Myths, Realities and Prospects.*

13. Said Chikhi, Algeria. *From Mass Rebellion to Workers' Protest.*

14. Bertil Odén, *Namibia's Economic Links to South Africa.*

1992

15. Cervenka Zdenek, *African National Congress Meets Eastern Europe. A Dialogue on Common Experiences.*

1993

16. Diallo Garba, *Mauritania–The Other Apartheid?*

1994

17. Zdenek Cervenka and Colin Legum, *Can National Dialogue Break the Power of Terror in Burundi?*

18. Erik Nordberg and Uno Winblad, *Urban Environmental Health and Hygiene in Sub-Saharan Africa.*

1996

19. Chris Dunton and Mai Palmberg, *Human Rights and Homosexuality in Southern Africa.*

1998

20. Georges Nzongola-Ntalaja, *From Zaire to the Democratic Republic of the Congo.*

1999

21. Filip Reyntjens, *Talking or Fighting? Political Evolution in Rwanda and Burundi, 1998–1999.*

22. Herbert Weiss, *War and Peace in the Democratic Republic of the Congo.*

2000

23. Filip Reyntjens, *Small States in an Unstable Region – Rwanda and Burundi, 1999–2000.*

2001

24. Filip Reyntjens, *Again at the Crossroads: Rwanda and Burundi, 2000–2001.*

25. Henning Melber, *The New African Initiative and the African Union. A Preliminary Assessment and Documentation.*

2003

26. Dahilon Yassin Mohamoda, *Nile Basin Cooperation. A Review of the Literature.*

2004

27. Henning Melber (ed.), *Media, Public Discourse and Political Contestation in Zimbabwe.*

28. Georges Nzongola-Ntalaja, *From Zaire to the Democratic Republic of the Congo.* (Second and Revised Edition)

2005

29. Henning Melber (ed.), *Trade, Development, Cooperation – What Future for Africa?*

30. Kaniye S.A. Ebeku, *The Succession of Faure Gnassingbe to the Togolese Presidency – An International Law Perspective.*

31. J.V. Lazarus, C. Christiansen, L. Rosendal Østergaard, L.A. Richey, Models for Life – Advancing antiretroviral therapy in sub-Saharan Africa.

2006

32. Charles Manga Fombad & Zein Kebonang, *AU, NEPAD and the APRM – Democratisation Efforts Explored.* (Ed. H. Melber.)

33. P.P. Leite, C. Olsson, M. Schöldtz, T. Shelley, P. Wrange, H. Corell and K. Scheele, *The Western Sahara Conflict – The Role of Natural Resources in Decolonization.* (Ed. Claes Olsson)

2007

34. Jassey, Katja and Stella Nyanzi, *How to Be a "Proper" Woman in the Times of HIV and AIDS.*

35. M. Lee, H. Melber, S. Naidu and I. Taylor, *China in Africa.* (Compiled by Henning Melber)

36. Nathaniel King, *Conflict as Integration. Youth Aspiration to Personhood in the Teleology of Sierra Leone's 'Senseless War'.*

2008

37. Aderanti Adepoju, *Migration in sub-Saharan Africa.*

38. Bo Malmberg, *Demography and the development potential of sub-Saharan Africa.*

39. Johan Holmberg, *Natural resources in sub-Saharan Africa: Assets and vulnerabilities.*

40. Arne Bigsten and Dick Durevall, *The African economy and its role in the world economy.*

41. Fantu Cheru, *Africa's development in the 21st century: Reshaping the research agenda.*

2009

42. Dan Kuwali, *Persuasive Prevention. Towards a Principle for Implementing Article 4(h) and R2P by the African Union.*

43. Daniel Volman, *China, India, Russia and the United States. The Scramble for African Oil and the Militarization of the Continent.*

2010

44. Mats Hårsmar, *Understanding Poverty in Africa? A Navigation through Disputed Concepts, Data and Terrains.*

2011

45. Sam Maghimbi, Razack B. Lokina and Mathew A. Senga, *The Agrarian Question in Tanzania? A State of the Art Paper.*

46. William Minter, *African Migration, Global Inequalities, and Human Rights. Connecting the Dots.*

47. Musa Abutudu and Dauda Garuba, *Natural Resource Governance and EITI Implementation in Nigeria.*

48. Ilda Lindell, *Transnational Activism Networks and Gendered Gatekeeping. Negotiating Gender in an African Association of Informal Workers.*

2012

49. Terje Oestigaard, *Water Scarcity and Food Security along the Nile. Politics, population increase and climate change.*

50. David Ross Olanya, *From Global Land Grabbing for Biofuels to Acquisitions of AfricanWater for Commercial Agriculture.*

2013

51. Gessesse Dessie, *Favouring a Demonised Plant. Khat and Ethiopian smallholder enterprise.*

52. Boima Tucker, *Musical Violence. Gangsta Rap and Politics in Sierra Leone.*